Jeanne Baudot en disant : Tout le monde
connaît mon faible pour elle.

Dimanche 29 Janvier. — Nous
allons avec Jeanne voir la collection
Pellerin. Je ne comprends rien à cet
homme qui n'y connaît rien en peinture
et paraît cependant avoir une adoration
pour le talent de mon oncle Edouard
dont il a des choses superbes : Leon Leenoff
en couleurs devant une table couverte
de quantités de choses si admirablement
peintes, Nana, la femme en Espagne couchée
sur un canapé que je ne connaissais pas
et qui est admirableuse, quelle peinture !
puis le skating, le bar, l'artiste que
j'aime moins ; une femme une dont Pellerin
est enchanté et qui est belle en effet,
mais le fonds est d'un noir qui
m'étonne, puis des esquisses, de petites
choses un homme suicidé impressionnant de

GROWING UP WITH THE
IMPRESSIONISTS

The Diary of Julie Manet

GROWING UP WITH THE

IMPRESSIONISTS

The Diary of Julie Manet

Translated, edited, and with an introduction
by Rosalind de Boland Roberts and
Jane Roberts

Sotheby's Publications

To Clément Rouart

The authors would like to thank all the members of the Rouart family for their help with the research on this book. In particular we acknowledge our special debt to Madame Agathe Valéry-Rouart and Monsieur Jean Griot who were able to impart their valuable personal memories of the Manet, Rouart, Valéry and Baudot families. We would also like to record our thanks to Monsieur André Chadefaux for his photographic work. Finally, we are most grateful to Charles Stuckey for his invaluable practical advice and encouragement during the preparation of this book.

FRONTISPIECE
Pierre Auguste Renoir *Berthe Morisot and her daughter Julie in 1894. Berthe Morisot was deeply affected by her husband's death and aged considerably in a very short period, her hair becoming white almost overnight*

© 1987 Diary text: Rosalind de Boland Roberts
© 1987 Introductory text and notes—Rosalind de Boland Roberts and Jane Roberts

First published 1987 for Sotheby's Publications
by Philip Wilson Publishers Ltd, 26 Litchfield Street, London WC2H 9NJ

Distributed in the USA by Sotheby's Publications, Harper & Row, Publishers, Inc
10 East 53rd Street, New York, NY 10022

ISBN 0 85667 340 4

Designed by Gillian Greenwood
Phototypeset by Tradespools Ltd, Frome, Somerset
Printed and bound in England by
BAS Printers, Over Wallop, Nr Stockbridge, Hampshire

Contents

1898

1899

Envoi

Julie Manet *The dovecot at Le Mesnil*

Berthe Morisot and her husband Eugène Manet with their daughter Julie, aged about 2, in the garden at Bougival

Introduction

'To record one's thoughts every day is an excellent idea; nothing forms one's style more effectively. And by this I mean not the habit of turning out fine phrases but of putting one's thoughts into words. It even seems to me that we ought to be very lenient, to condone lack of correctness, provided that the feeling is real and that the ideas are personal', wrote Berthe Morisot in 1884 to her sister Edma who had sent her the diary of her eldest daughter.[1]

Many young girls write diaries and it is hardly surprising that, with her mother holding such views and giving encouragement, Julie Manet would prove to be no exception to the rule. Indeed, at the tender age of ten, we read that Julie is writing her memoirs and learning to play the mandolin.[2] However this was a short-lived attempt and it wasn't until 1893 that Julie began her diary in earnest. This was not to be a neat ladylike leather bound volume but untidy notes scribbled down in old exercise books, often in pencil, the presentation as spontaneous as the contents. It is a vivid depiction of a vital period in France's cultural history seen through the youthful but surprisingly perspicacious eyes of the youngest member of what was surely one of the most prominent artistic families of the time.

Julie Manet was born in Paris on 14 November 1878 into this wealthy and cultured milieu at the height of the Impressionist era. In many ways she had a rather conventional but extremely happy childhood, loved and cherished by adoring and artistic parents and relatives. Her diary recounts cloudless summers with seemingly endless numbers of trips to interesting places and Parisian winters crammed with concerts and exhibitions. But this was no ordinary family or circle of friends: Julie lived among and painted with the most influential and important artists of the period. Her sailing trips were with the poet Mallarmé, her picnics with the painter Renoir, and her visits to the Louvre with Degas. And we read, as the diary closes, how Paul Valéry courted (and later married) her first cousin, Jeannie.

Julie was the only child of the painter Berthe Morisot and her husband Eugène Manet, the younger brother of Edouard Manet, the most controversial artist of the day. By the time she began her *Journal* the Impressionists were well known if not always respected, middle aged, and already going their different ways artistically. They remained, however, surprisingly close and friendly and provided her with a loving and supportive circle when she was left an orphan in 1895.

Julie's unique background inevitably led to the formation of her own talent and the development of her striking powers of observation. Her childhood had been steeped in the arts from the very start and, surrounded by her parents' circle of friends, which included many of the greatest artists of the time, she grew up in a rarefied atmosphere of painting, music, and literary conversation, which prompted an early maturity and an inquiring, perceptive mind.

Berthe Morisot, born in 1841, was an experienced and serious painter by the time she married in 1874, only a few months after she had exhibited four paintings, two pastels, and three watercolours in the first Impressionist exhibition held at the photographer Nadar's studio in the Boulevard des Capucines. Berthe had always been encouraged by her family to paint but what had begun as a required and ladylike pastime had for her become a lifelong passion and serious career, while her two sisters, Yves and Edma, had given up painting when they married or before.

The Morisot family was distantly related by marriage to the eighteenth-century painter Fragonard, and the young Morisot ladies certainly had an artistic and creative bent which was recognized and fostered by their parents. Their father, Tiburce, had trained as an architect but abandoned this profession for a more respectable and lucrative career in administration. The three sisters began painting lessons in 1857 with a mediocre Academician, Chocarne, copying old masters in the Louvre, but later received a solid grounding in studio drawing and technique from their teacher Guichard, the Lyonnais artist, who was an enlightened pupil of

Ingres and Delacroix. Guichard was quick to realize that these young ladies had far more than the necessary social accomplishment in painting and told their mother that, with the talent they possessed, they would inevitably become painters. 'Do you realize what this means?' he asked Madame Morisot. 'In your bourgeois environment this will be a revolution, I might almost say a catastrophe!'[3] Eventually, since Berthe insisted on pursuing her studies in front of the motif *en plein air*, observing nature first hand, Guichard reluctantly surrendered his pupils to Corot.

For the next two years Berthe and Edma worked under Corot, who soon became a friend of the Morisot household, where he dined each Tuesday. It was quite adventurous and highly unconventional for young ladies to spend summers travelling on mule and horseback in the Pyrenees, sketching and painting in the open air, but this is how the two girls spent the summer of 1862.[4] There is no doubt that Berthe had her mother's support in her artistic endeavours and that there was absolutely no opposition from her family as she became increasingly committed to painting. Family holidays were organized around her desire to paint outdoors and both parents encouraged visits from artists such as Carolus Duran and Alfred Stevens.

In 1868, while on one of her frequent visits to the Louvre with her friend Rosalie Riesener, Berthe Morisot was introduced to Edouard Manet by the painter Henri Fantin-Latour. Berthe had been wanting to meet Manet for some time and their attraction to each other was spontaneous and long lasting. The Morisots and the Manets soon formed close ties, which were to result not only in Berthe's marriage to Eugène but in a fruitful artistic exchange until Edouard Manet's death in 1883. Berthe served as his model as early as 1869 for LE BALCON and LE REPOS, and for her favourite portrait by Manet, BERTHE MORISOT AU BOUQUET DE VIOLETTES, painted in 1872, which she bought when it came under the hammer at the Duret sale at the Galerie Georges Petit in March 1894; it still hangs in her Paris home to this day.

Berthe Morisot was never a pupil of Manet (his only pupil was the painter Eva Gonzalès)[5] but Berthe and Manet nevertheless were in constant contact and their influence on each other's work cannot be underestimated. Manet could not dissuade her from joining the Impressionist group formed in 1873, which he believed to be a futile venture. 'The Salon is the real field of battle; these little arenas bore me so!'[6] But Berthe was impressed by Monet and Degas, whom she had met at her mother's famous Thursday evening soirées at which there was much stimulating conversation from artists and writers like Zola, Puvis de Chavannes, Zacharie Astruc and Fantin-Latour, while Madame Manet (Julie's 'Tante Suzanne') played the piano.

The year 1874 marked another step forward in Berthe's career and a change in her relationship with Manet. A group of young artists, including Monet, Renoir, Sisley, and Degas (although he had certain reservations), had agreed on the principle of abandoning the Salon and had formed a limited group with the aim of mounting their own exhibitions. Berthe was one of the first to join them and undertook to submit no more work to the official Salon jury. She exhibited constantly at all the 'Impressionist' shows thereafter, except one, in 1879, the year after Julie was born.

Edouard Manet had written to Fantin-Latour on 26 August 1868: 'I totally agree with you... The Misses Morisot are delightful; it's just a pity that they don't happen to be men. However I suppose they could as women serve the cause of Painting by marrying Academicians and give the Old Buffers a shock. Come to think of it, that might be asking a bit much of them! Meanwhile, please send them my regards.'[7] But Manet had no need to underestimate the talent or determination of Berthe; she worked as hard as any man and became as important a member of the Impressionist group as Monet or Sisley. Indeed, there is evidence to show that Manet himself valued her opinion of his own work very highly.

Berthe married Eugène Manet, Edouard's younger brother, in December 1874 at the Eglise de Passy. She had spent the years of the Franco-Prussian war in Paris with her parents and later suffered, like all Parisians, the upheaval of the Commune. Her health was poor but she had not stopped working. She was also the only unmarried Mademoiselle Morisot left since Yves had married Théodore Gobillard, a tax official from Quimperlé in 1867, and Edma had married Adolphe Pontillon, a naval officer based at Lorient in 1869. After her father's death in January 1874 Berthe had moved with her mother to a smaller apartment in the Rue Guichard. Sadly little is known about Eugène apart from the fact that he was a frequent model for his brother and posed for the notorious DÉJEUNER SUR L'HERBE. He himself seems to have been a quiet, rather self-effacing man who was always subject to ill-health and who did not have a profession (family wealth meant that there was no need for any of the Manet brothers to work).

Marriage did not change Berthe Morisot's way of life or her artistic career; the couple lived until her mother's death in 1876 with Mme Morisot and then moved to an apartment at 9 Avenue d'Eylau. Summers were spent visiting relatives or travelling to places of interest, as in 1875 when she and her husband visited England and stayed on the Isle of Wight. While on these travels she worked hard, sketching and even painting full-scale canvases. Her husband used to accompany her and he himself liked to work in pastels, of which there are few examples left. Indeed Eugène was invited to exhibit with the Impressionist group at their 1877 show but, ever modest, he declined to do so. Nevertheless he spent a great deal of time in assisting with the preparations for exhibitions (he prepared the catalogue and arranged the hanging of their first exhibition in 1874) and in giving them his support.

Berthe Morisot was discreet about her work. She never had a special atelier, even when the couple had a house built for them in the Rue de Villejust. She would work all day in the cathedral-like drawing-room, hiding her paints and brushes behind a screen once she had finished. She was ever open to and interested in new ideas and techniques, as in 1888, when Julie was given a present of a box of coloured crayons, these were quickly adopted by Berthe and became a very personal means of expression. She always remained a *grande bourgeoise* and was without the Bohemian traits of many of her contemporaries. Indeed her best friends, Degas, Monet, and Edouard Manet, were far from being what we think of as starving artists in garrets, living *la vie de Bohème*. Only Renoir and later Monet had serious financial problems, but by the time Julie was a teenager they all led calm, hardworking middle-class lives.

Julie's arrival on 14 November 1878 temporarily interrupted her mother's career as an exhibitor with the Impressionists. One may suppose that having a first baby at thirty-seven, when her health was far from good, must have been an ordeal for Berthe Morisot, but it was one which she certainly never regretted—though, in a humorous letter to her sister Yves, Berthe seems to have had a few reservations about the appearance of her new-born baby daughter. 'Well, I am just like everybody else! I regret that Bibi is not a boy. In the first place because she looks like a boy; then, she would perpetuate a famous name; and mostly for the simple reason that each and every one of us, men and women, are in love with the male sex. . . Your Bibi is a darling; you'll find mine ugly in comparison, with her head as flat as a paving stone. . . All poor Julie has to offer is her fat cheeks and her pretty complexion.' And in another letter to Yves: 'Julie or Rose is like a big inflated balloon. . . . My daughter is a Manet to the tips of her fingers; even at this early date she is like her uncles, she has nothing of me.'[8] Nevertheless Julie was her mother's inspiration and her favourite model. From the cradle until she became a self-assured young girl there are countless images of her in every kind of mood and occupation.

Berthe Morisot's atelier in the drawing-room of 40 Rue de Villejust

Eugène Manet
*Studies of Berthe
Morisot and Julie*

Berthe Morisot
Julie and her doll

Berthe Morisot *Julie feeding the ducks in the Bois de Boulogne*

Julie must have had an idyllic childhood, spending summers in Bougival where Berthe and her husband had rented a villa at 4 Rue de la Princesse, which they had found in 1881. The banks of the Seine around Rueil and Croissy were favourite haunts of the Impressionists: Manet at Rueil, Renoir and Sisley at Louveciennes, Pissarro at Marly, all depicted the lazy and tranquil atmosphere of what is now no more than a suburb of Paris but which was then a bucolic haven for artists.

Getting away from the city in the summer is still a necessary and beneficial tradition among Parisians, but was even more so in the case of the Eugène Manets during 1881, 1882, and 1883 because they were having a large town house built on a piece of land they had bought previously on the Rue de Villejust, near the Etoile. On the ground floor it would have a high-ceilinged atelier-style drawing-room (inspired by a church in Nice which had caught Berthe's eye) and which would be her workplace; the four storeys above that would house, on various floors and at different times, Julie and her cousins, Julie and her husband, and cousin Jeannie and her husband Paul Valéry—indeed the building houses a son and grandsons of Julie Manet to this day.

Berthe and her husband at last had enough room to entertain their large circle— the friends and acquaintances who were to affect Julie's upbringing and look after her so well once both her parents were dead. Eugène's health was far from good and Berthe's weekly salons were a source of distraction and entertainment for him since he rarely left the house. They became as renowned as her mother's soirées had been, but now the guests included the Symbolist poet Mallarmé, Monet, Degas, Caillebotte, Renoir, Puvis de Chavannes and even Whistler on occasion. Berthe Morisot's salons were not only occasions when visitors were entertained but times when writers and artists could meet each other. There was one particularly memorable evening in 1890 when Mallarmé gave his famous *Conférence sur Villiers de l'Isle-Adam*,[9] before an invited audience of between thirty and forty people including de Régnier, Dujardin, de Wyzewa, Madame and Geneviève Mallarmé and, of course, Julie and her cousins Paule and Jeannie Gobillard. The lecture went

Berthe Morisot *Julie and her nursemaid on the balcony at 4 Rue de la Princesse, Bougival*

Berthe Morisot *Bronze bust of Julie Manet. This is the only sculpture by Berthe Morisot and it is said that she asked Rodin for technical advice when working on it*

down very well, except with Degas who, irritable and short tempered, was unable to hide his impatience and stalked out of the room muttering that he couldn't understand a word of it.[10]

Julie was allowed, even as a young child, to sit at the 'big table' and listen to all these eminent grown-ups, and she was certainly trained from an extremely early age to look at things with a painter's eyes. (We can see this clearly in her *Journal*.) Her mother took her on trips abroad and encouraged her to visit museums and places of cultural interest. Julie had visited Italy, Belgium, and Holland with her parents and spent a summer in Jersey by the time she was eight. Her mother's constant work must have been an encouragement to her to start drawing and painting herself and this she seems to have done at a very early age.

In 1887 Berthe Morisot executed the only bronze she is known to have made, a bust of Julie, for which she had to ask for technical help from the sculptor Rodin. The work shows a determined-looking child with a near perfect oval face and pigtail.

While Julie was growing into a healthy and inquiring young girl, her father's health was fast declining. In 1890 the family spent six months in the country at Le Mézy in the valley of the Seine, and, finding the country air beneficial to his

La Maison Blotière at Le Mézy—Berthe Morisot and her ailing husband spent several summers in this house beside the Seine. It was while staying here that they discovered the château at Le Mesnil, a few miles away, which was to become their property in 1892

The Château du Mesnil-Saint-Laurent, overlooking the Seine

condition, they returned there the following year. It was during a long leisurely ramble one summer afternoon that they caught a glimpse of a beautiful seventeenth-century château, surrounded by outhouses and extensive grounds, the Château du Mesnil Saint-Laurent, between Meulan and Mantes. Renoir had told them about this jewel, and needless to say Berthe and her husband fell in love with it. 'We have not bought a château; there is one for sale near the village, so extraordinarily cheap that for a moment we had the idea of committing this folly. It is extremely pretty. Eugène was crazy about it and Julie too. But we will be reasonable; the house in Paris is quite enough', Berthe wrote to Edma in August 1891. But on 29 September she was writing to Mallarmé that 'the deal was off, but now it is on again'.[11] The purchase was a lengthy process and it was not until the winter of 1892 after many hesitations that it was completed. Neither Berthe nor her husband were to live there for any length of time and it was let for 2,500 francs

Julie Manet (on the left) sitting next to Jeannie Gobillard who is holding Paul Valéry's hand; at the easel, Paule Gobillard and a friend. This photograph was taken in the third-floor apartment at the Rue de Villejust which Julie, Jeannie, and Paule occupied after Berthe Morisot's death

immediately after Eugène's death because Berthe Morisot never wanted to live at Le Mesnil again. 'It was certainly a find and I have a great satisfaction thinking that some day Julie will enjoy it and fill it with her children. But as for myself, I feel mortally sad in it, and am in a hurry to leave.'[12] Indeed it was later to become Julie's home and to be the centre of her life with her husband Ernest Rouart and their three sons.

In 1892 Julie lost her father, to whom she was exceptionally attached. Berthe Morisot, who had nursed him through the last months of his life, was grief-stricken and was never to recover fully from the loss. She wrote to a friend: 'I am ending my life in the widowhood you experienced as a young woman. I do not say loneliness, since I have Julie, but it is a kind of solitude none the less, for, instead of opening my heart, I must control myself and spare her tender years the sight of my grief.'[13] Renoir's portrait of Berthe and Julie, painted in 1894, is particularly telling. Berthe has become white-haired practically overnight. She has a world-weary expression and doesn't seem to be able to face the artist but looks away sadly, leaving the limelight to Julie (who was sixteen and exceptionally pretty). Julie's childhood and adolescence were to be saddened by a succession of deaths of friends and relatives to add to her grief for her father. In her diary she often reflects on death in a most mature way for such a young girl; her optimism and resilience when confronted with these painful losses seem remarkable.

So Julie became her mother's even closer and more constant companion, and it was in 1893 that she began to write her diary. Her admiration for Berthe knew no bounds and she recorded her remarks and thoughts in great and loving detail. It was in this year too that Julie and her mother moved from the Rue de Villejust to a much smaller apartment at 10 Rue Weber. Berthe Morisot must have sensed that her own health was fragile because in April 1892 she named Stéphane Mallarmé as Julie's guardian and created a family council to look after Julie should any misfortune befall her.

Julie's mother's death in 1895 was more sudden and brutal than her father's had been as Julie had always known him as an invalid. While nursing her ailing daughter Berthe caught influenza, which quickly turned into pneumonia. She died on 2 March, leaving a poignant letter in which she took leave of her beloved daughter.[14]

Julie was orphaned but, though the future appeared uncertain and bleak, an unusual solution to her problems was to prove very successful. Her cousins Paule and Jeannie Gobillard, who had also been left alone when their mother, the former Yves Morisot, died in 1893, were living on the third floor of the house in the Rue de Villejust. It was agreed by the *conseil de famille* and Mallarmé that Julie should join them and that the three girls should live there together with a suitable house-keeper, found by Mallarmé, who was installed to keep an eye on this youthful, feminine household. Julie pursued her painting and academic studies and was allowed as much freedom as a young lady of the period would expect to visit friends, go to concerts, and to enjoy Parisian life. As an only child she was especially close to her first cousins. Paule Gobillard, who was to become an

Berthe Morisot *Julie and Jeannie Gobillard playing the flute*

accomplished artist, was twelve years older than Julie but the younger girl, Jeannie, was virtually her contemporary. Paule would always remain a maiden aunt figure. Having watched over Julie and her own younger sister as well as Edma Morisot's daughters Blanche and Jeanne Pontillon for many years, she pursued her career and was always a great favourite with her nephews and nieces.

Julie seems to have had a somewhat haphazard education. Various lessons were shared with Jeannie; various governesses attempted to teach them the rudiments of French literature and English. Berthe Morisot had modern ideas on education and advised 'controlled' freedom as far as reading matter was considered. 'If I were you I would be particular in the choice of reading—no drivel, nothing sentimental, nothing affected, as many good old French authors as possible. We are all born monkeys before we are ourselves; therein lies the danger of bad examples.'[15] Julie read a lot, although she claims the contrary in her diary—mainly books recommended by Mallarmé, Renoir, and Degas; also she seems to have had a precocious penchant for adult reading matter—a fact hardly surprising for the only daughter of middle-aged parents constantly surrounded by adults, and exceptional ones at that. She enjoyed Edgar Allan Poe but found Delacroix's *Journal* a little tedious. Berthe Morisot had seen to it that her daughter received the required schooling but there is no doubt that Julie's heart was elsewhere; she was already devoted to art and painting, and her only desire was to become an artist like her mother and most of the friends who surrounded her. Apart from art her other lasting passion was music.

Berthe Morisot had been very fond of classical music and this taste she shared with most of her artist friends. Renoir was exceptionally attracted to opera, with a special taste for Wagner. He painted Wagner's portrait and admired his music, although his pupil, the artist Jeanne Baudot, recounts that on a visit to Bayreuth in 1896 with his friend Caillebotte he became fidgety and bored during a lengthy performance of *Parsifal* and had the audacity to strike a match so that he could look at his watch.[16] Degas obviously enjoyed going to concerts and ballets, but it was Mallarmé who really shared Berthe's love of music. She usually attended a concert on Sunday afternoons with Julie, often the Concerts Lamoureux or Concerts Colonne. Sometimes they would meet Mallarmé in the promenade galleries, where he would be making copious notes in a little book he always carried. They would stroll up the Champs-Elysées afterwards discussing the afternoon's performance as they went.

It was natural that Julie should take up an instrument and she not only played the flute and the piano but became quite masterly on the violin (there are many studies by her mother of Julie playing musical instruments).

Julie spent many hours practising and received weekly lessons in musical theory, composition, and appreciation from assorted music teachers—lessons which she shared with her cousin Jeannie Gobillard who was to become a pianist of professional standard. Her favourite teacher was without doubt the young Jules Boucherit, of whom she often wrote in her diary, and one can detect that a young girl of sixteen or so might even have felt a slight romantic *frisson* when she heard this handsome young maestro play with such passion. The girls often prepared musical entertainments and soirées for their friends and seem to have attempted quite difficult pieces, though preferring Berlioz, Gounod, Mendelssohn and Schumann to the more avant-garde music of their day (Julie was puzzled by Wagner). Also Chabrier was a great favourite, but there might have been a little *parti-pris* here since Berthe Morisot was one of his greatest friends and admirers. One thing is certain: Julie rarely felt indifferent about music and she always had firm opinions, whether on the interpretation or on the music itself.

In fact Julie seems to have been a very well-informed young lady altogether, keeping up with current affairs, listening with curiosity to the different opinions of her mother's friends, and reaching her own conclusions. We see this particularly during the Dreyfus Affair which had become a *cause célèbre* by 1896, a year after her mother's death, and which was shaking France to the core.

It is difficult to imagine the impact that the case of Alfred Dreyfus had on the French population at all levels at that time. *L'Affaire Dreyfus* was, of course, just the culminating event in more than twenty years of anti-semitic activity in France, linked with anti-German feeling (after the Franco-Prussian war of 1870–71) and a marked fear of being overrun by foreigners. Various publications reflected this anti-semitic thinking. *La France Juive*, published by Drumont, and the more virulent *L'Intransigeant*, a periodical edited by the anti-semite Henri Rochefort, were both widely read, as was *La Libre Parole*, whose subtitle was 'France for the French'. As well as publications, there were the rather pitiful royalist and right extremist Boulangist movement and the more determined creation in 1890 of the *Ligue Anti-sémite Nationale Française*.

By the mid 1890s the French had been bombarded by the press with the notions that all evil revolutionaries or corrupt bankers were Jews and that Jews had been responsible for the misfortunes of France ever since the Franco-Prussian war. The French looked around them to find that Jews did indeed dominate the financial, intellectual, and scientific spheres in the country. Great families who considered

Berthe Morisot *'A music lesson'*
Jeannie Gobillard and Julie Manet with their
teacher Jules Boucherit

themselves to be more French than the French, such as the Halévys, the Haas, the Schlumbergers, the Camondos, the Ephrussis and the Rothschilds were suddenly viewed with suspicion and thought to be desiring one thing—the ruin of France. It was in this racist and nationalistic atmosphere, which was explosive to say the least, that the Dreyfus Affair was headline news throughout France. To our eyes it all seems a little ludicrous: On 26 September 1894 a Parisian cleaning woman who was regularly paid by the French secret service to keep an eye on the waste-paper baskets of the German Embassy discovered a *bordereau* (or list) of strategic details concerning French troops along the Alsatian border. This discovery suggested the information was being leaked by a French officer from the War Office and, after a very sketchy investigation, suspicion settled on Captain Alfred Dreyfus, a brilliant but unpopular career officer who also happened to be an Alsatian and a Jew. He was arrested, accused, found guilty of high treason, and in December was sentenced to life imprisonment on Devil's Island. The majority in France applauded the judges and approved of the harsh sentence, but his family and many thinkers were convinced of his innocence, realizing that he had been convicted on very slender evidence. When in 1896 evidence pointing to the guilt of another officer, Esterhazy, came to light, the Dreyfus supporters, including Monet and his friends Clemenceau and Emile Zola, launched a massive campaign demanding a re-trial of Dreyfus.

However, the accusations against Esterhazy resulted in his acquittal by court-martial in January 1898. In protest against the verdict Zola published his famous letter '*J'accuse*' in Clemenceau's newspaper *L'Aurore* on 13 January. In it he attacked the army for concealing proofs of the innocence of Dreyfus and with failing to convict Esterhazy—an action for which Zola and the manager of the paper were tried and found guilty of libel; after which Zola, on the advice of friends, fled to England.

The country was divided into two distinct camps: the Dreyfusards, who favoured a revision of the trial and believed an innocent man had been sent to prison—a group which included Monet, Proust, Jacques-Emile Blanche, Thadée Natanson, Pissarro and, of course, Zola. The anti-Dreyfusards included Degas, Paul Valéry, Alexis Rouart, Henri Rouart and his four sons, Forain and Cézanne among many others who were sometimes naïvely nationalistic but first and foremost felt passionately French. Terrible quarrels ensued. Degas, for example, fell out with the Halévys, the Camondos, and many other long-standing friends, Renoir apparently 'contrived to be non-committal'[17]. His son, Jean, in *Renoir, My Father*[18] quotes Renoir as declaiming: 'Always the same camps, but with different names for each century. Protestants against Catholics, Republicans against Royalists, Communards against the Versailles faction. The old quarrel has been revived again. People are either pro or anti Dreyfus. I would try to be simply a Frenchman.' But one can't help noticing the directness with which he attacks French Jewry in Julie's diary.

In fact the Manet family seems to have been surrounded by anti-Dreyfusards, and it is not surprising therefore that Julie relates Renoir's disobliging remarks about the pro-Dreyfus and Jewish Pissarro, and Degas' friends' rather biased opinions against Dreyfus. However it is interesting to note that at one stage she writes in her diary that it would be terrible if the French people condemned an innocent man.

In a much lighter vein, Julie also tells of the state visit of the Russian Tsar Nicholas II and his Empress to Paris in 1896. She describes the decorations and festivities organized by the people of Paris for this occasion and her enjoyment of the firework display, which was supposed to have been one of the most impressive ever staged in the capital. By no means blinded by the pomp and ceremony of the visit, Julie relates all the details with great humour and insight.

We can see from Julie's *Journal* that her parents' friends formed a supportive and generous circle on which she and her cousins could depend for their social life as well as their education. Mallarmé, behind his serious exterior and intellectual manner, was in fact an amusing companion. He had found a great friend in Berthe Morisot and, after her death, kept his word in becoming Julie's guardian. His wife and daughter Geneviève also kept an eye on the three girls, but it was Mallarmé who sent Julie little poems, took her to concerts, and invited her to stay at his country house at Valvins on the banks of the Seine. It was a terrible shock when he died suddenly in 1898. Julie was devastated by the loss but tried to comfort his widow and especially her close friend Geneviève.

There remained Monet, Degas, and, of course, Renoir, who had taken Julie on holiday to Brittany with his family a few months after Berthe's death. By the time Julie was made an orphan, Renoir had at long last married Aline Charigot,[19] thus recognizing their son Pierre (born in 1885). He had met Aline (who came from a little village called Essoyes in southern Champagne and who was a seamstress) as early as 1880 but, inclining towards an independent life, had spent much time since then travelling alone or with friends throughout Europe and North Africa. After the birth of their second son Jean in 1894 he seems to have led a more stable existence, sharing his time between a home in Paris at 13 Rue Girardon (known as the 'Château des Brouillards'), the south of France, where he visited Cézanne, and later at Essoyes. In 1893 he had met a doctor's daughter, Jeanne Baudot, who became his close friend and pupil and was godmother to his son Jean. He had naturally enough introduced her to Julie and her cousins and they would work together at the Louvre and receive advice—which was always gratefully accepted by the young artists—from the master. Julie painted Jeanne on many occasions and they remained life-long companions.

Of all the friends who looked after Julie when her parents died, Renoir seems to have been the most fun-loving and he enjoyed teasing Julie as much as Mallarmé had. He appears always to have been available when she needed help or advice and was less didactic and forbidding than Degas.

Julie visited the Monet household at Giverny on several occasions. Monet lived there with his second wife, Mme Alice Hoschedé, and the house was constantly filled with both his and her numerous children and grandchildren. Giverny's rooms were sparsely furnished in an avant-garde manner and the walls were painted with bright, striking colours that served as a marvellous background for Monet's collection of Japanese prints, pottery, and oriental rugs. Monet curiously kept a Cézanne in the bathroom as well as four Jongkinds, three Delacroix, a Degas, a Fantin-Latour, two Caillebottes, three Pissarros, and a Sisley; another twelve Cézannes, nine Renoirs, and five Berthe Morisots were placed in more conventional settings. Monet's studio, where he never painted, held a collection of his own paintings retracing every period of his life.[20] One can imagine that Julie enjoyed being invited to Giverny, where she would have enjoyed the company of other visitors, such as Rodin, Sargent, Durand-Ruel, Natanson, the Bernheims, and Clemenceau. Conversation would be about food and wine and especially the garden, which was Monet's main concern in the summer.

The Giverny household could not help being involved in the Dreyfus Affair as Monet was a fervent Dreyfusard and supported Zola, unlike most of Berthe Morisot's friends.

The most fervent anti-Dreyfusard seems to have been Degas. He became something of a recluse in his later years although he saw much of Julie and entertained her and her young cousins and their friends. He lived in an apartment in the Rue Victor-Massé with his house-keeper Zoë who would prepare simple but copious suppers for his friends (Julie describes one such occasion). In his old age Degas became crankier and more bad-tempered; he didn't approve of any new-fangled contraptions such as aeroplanes or even bicycles; he thought the telephone 'ridiculous', hated dogs and especially flowers (it was the smell rather than the colour that displeased him). Julie loved Degas as one loves a temperamental and old-fashioned uncle. He gave her much advice and was responsible for introducing her to her husband-to-be Ernest Rouart when one afternoon towards the end of 1898 he invited Julie to tea along with Ernest, one of his pupils. Degas suggested

Guests at Giverny, Monet's home, enjoying the beautiful gardens

light-heartedly that it would be a good idea if they got married, and we see in Julie's *Journal* that what began as a little joke later became a reality.

Degas wrote in 1900, after the couple were engaged to be married: 'We have Ernest, who after having been timid and cold is becoming nonchalant and hot. On Wednesday at about a quarter past seven he arrived on foot with Julie at his Uncle Alexis' home, with such a married air that you would have died laughing. "Already?" I asked. And what's more, Julie, who usually opens her mouth just a little bit more than him, seemed just as relaxed as he was. It's astonishing, as Monsieur Prud'homme along with me would say, how men and women are made for each other.'[21]

Indeed Degas had every reason to be pleased with his bit of matchmaking because, a few weeks before this letter, at a soirée at which Pablo Casals played, Paul Valéry became engaged to Julie's favourite cousin, Jeannie Gobillard, and in May 1900, at the parish church of Saint Honoré d'Eylau in the Passy district, Julie married Ernest Rouart and Paul Valéry married Jeannie in a double ceremony.

NOTES

1 *The Correspondence of Berthe Morisot*, Camden Press, London 1986, p. 139
2 ibid., p. 161
3 *The Correspondence of Berthe Morisot with her Family and Friends*, edited by Denis Rouart, Paris 1950, pp. 9–10
4 Rosamund Bernier, 'Dans la lumière impressionniste', in *L'Oeil*, Paris, May 1959, p. 40
5 There seems to have been a certain rivalry between the Morisot sisters and Eva Gonzalès, shown in a letter from Berthe to her sister Edma: 'Manet lectures me and holds up that eternal Mademoiselle Gonzalès as an example.' To which she replied: 'The thought of Mademoiselle Gonzalès irritates me, I do not know why. I imagine Manet greatly overestimates her, and that we, or rather you, have as much talent as she'—*Correspondence of Berthe Morisot*, Camden 1986, p. 44
6 Nathaniel Harris, *The Art of Manet*, London 1982, p. 58
7 E. Moreau-Nélaton, *Manet raconte par lui-même*, Laurens, Paris 1926, vol. I, pp. 102–3
8 *Correspondence of Berthe Morisot*, Camden 1986, p. 115
9 The conference on Villiers de l'Isle Adam took place on 24 February 1890
10 Henri Mondor, *La Vie de Stéphane Mallarmé*, Paris 1946, p. 574
11 *Correspondence of Berthe Morisot*, Camden 1986, pp. 184, 185
12 ibid., p. 194
13 ibid., p 197
14 see p. 61 in Julie's diary.
15 *Correspondence of Berthe Morisot*, Camden 1986, p. 139
16 Jeanne Baudot, *Renoir, ses amis, ses modèles*, Editions Littéraires de France, Paris 1949, pp. 77–9
17 see R.H. Wilenski, *Modern French Painters*, Faber, London 1940, p. 157
18 Jean Renoir, *Renoir, My Father*, Collins, London 1962, p. 229
19 Renoir married Aline Charigot on 14 April 1890
20 Claire Joyes, Andrew Forge, Jean-Marie Toulgouat and Robert Gordon, *Monet at Giverny*, Mathews Miller Dunbar, London 1975, pp. 15–23
21 Roy McMullen, *Degas: his Life, Times and Work*, Secker & Warburg, London 1985, p. 445

1893

Berthe Morisot *Portrait of Julie Manet and greyhound Laërtes, her favourite pet and a gift from Mallarmé*

'I have always wanted to keep a diary, so I think I'll start one now. I suppose I might have left it rather late. But the longer I wait, the later it will be—and after all I'm only fourteen.'

Mallarmé, the great Symbolist poet of the nineteenth century, aged about 43 years

Mallarmé's wife, Marie Gerhard, of German extraction. This picture was taken in the late sixties, when Mallarmé was teaching English in Avignon

OPPOSITE
Mallarmé's country house in Valvins, on the edge of the Seine and the Forêt de Fontainebleau. After his son's death in 1879, he spent more and more time there and was often to be seen sailing nearby

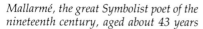

Thursday 24th August

This morning we got ready to go to Fontainebleau. We left at 2 o'clock, crossed Paris, and arrived at the Gare de Lyon with Octavie [Julie's maid], who'd come to take Laërtes back if they wouldn't allow him on to the train with us. However we found a compartment for passengers with dogs.

The train set off, going past Charenton, and we glimpsed the lovely greenish colour of the Marne; then saw a small lake or pond as blue as the Mediterranean.

We arrived at Fontainebleau at half past four, and left our things at the Valvins Hotel; then went to see M. Mallarmé, who is staying on the other side of the bridge, for the hotel at Valvins-les-Bains as it is called is on the banks of the Seine. Monsieur Mallarmé took us to where the forest begins. Madame and Mlle Mallarmé were there and we dined outdoors in front of the inn under some trees beside the Seine. I went to bed in a tiny room with a view over the river.

Sunday 27th August

We came back to Valvins [from Fontainebleau] in a magnificent four-seater carriage with cushions of white silk. In the afternoon we continued our paintings of views from the window, and towards 5 o'clock we went out and met M. Mallarmé on the road which goes down to the inn. He was with two young people who had come to see him; one an actor and friend of Rossignol; the other Camille Mauclair, who looked very fine, with hair sweeping his forehead.

Monsieur Mallarmé pointed out the road for Fontainebleau and sent them on their way; then we went to sit down with him on a bench in front of his house. Madame and Mlle Mallarmé had gone to Samois to pay a visit in a little carriage they had hired for the day. When Mlle Geneviève got back, I went for a short walk with her. She took me to Vulaines. There are lots of flowers in the village and the church is surrounded by juniper bushes, little firs, and green trees. We came back by a road through some vineyards with a fine view of the forest. She was wearing a green checked dress and a big hat with streamers.

Maman and I went back to the inn for dinner. We were afraid that the inn would be crowded, as it was on Thursday evening when some young people dining at the water's edge sang songs out of tune the whole time and made a frightful noise blowing hunting horns horribly badly between each course. (The service is very slow and they even contrived yesterday not to give us what was on the menu, but Maman complained to the proprietor and now it is much improved.) From my bed I watched a firework display on the other side of the Seine.

Berthe Morisot and her daughter spent most of their time at Valvins painting and going for walks and outings by carriage with the Mallarmé family.

Wednesday 30th August

We spent the morning painting in the forest near the road where we were yesterday. After lunch we went by carriage to fetch M., Madame, and Mlle Mallarmé. Maman, M., and Madame Mallarmé went in the big carriage and I went with Mlle Geneviève in hers. She has hired quite a nice horse for a month as from yesterday. We took Laërtes with us at first, but he made the most frightful noise so had to go in the big carriage. We went for a lovely outing. First we went to Queen Amélie's look-out, then to the calvary at the Roche Eponge from where one has a view of Fontainebleau. We came back by the Fonteau woods, where there are magnificent trees, and saw an oak and a beech growing from the same base and other oddities like that.

Laërtes was rather nervous and at every turn in the road he looked to see if our carriage was still behind. From far away, one couldn't tell what he was—he looked

Mallarmé's sailing-boat on the Seine—a scene often painted by Berthe Morisot and her daughter. Mallarmé is on the right of Thadée Natanson (photograph taken by Julie Manet in 1896)

rather like a bird. I went with Mlle Geneviève as far as their house and tried to unharness the horse with her, but I wasn't much help. Then she took me back. She's really very friendly, talks to me all the time, and doesn't seem to look down on little girls of fourteen. She even said I could call her Geneviève.

Laërtes, who likes her very much, didn't want to leave her. When he heard Maman arriving, he almost jumped through the window. I think his carriage ride has made him quite peculiar.

Thursday 31st August

We painted in the forest in the morning. In the afternoon M. Mallarmé came to invite Maman to go boating and Maman accepted the invitation. M. Mallarmé's boat is varnished and the bottom is light green; the sail is a lovely shape with a little flag above on which is S.M.

Friday 1st September

This morning we went for a delightful walk to Thoméry. We followed the Seine as far as the village, sometimes walking beneath the trees, sometimes out in the sunshine, through the grass filled with meadow-saffron, mallows, mint, and other pretty flowers. We passed by a large property with magnificent trees. Near the little path which we were following, some willows were mirrored in the Seine in which are lilies and other water flowers. Opposite one can see Samoreau and its little hill. We came back by the same route and I brought a lovely bunch of flowers with me. In the afternoon it rained a little, so we did some watercolours from our windows.

Maman is painting two blonde sisters who are very sweet. The older one must be sixteen and the other eleven. The first always wears blue and the second pink. They have berets or big straw hats and seem to adore their father; but as for their mother she spends the whole day fishing and seems to think of nothing else but her fish.

Saturday 2nd September

This morning we finished our studies in the forest and in the afternoon went to the Château de Fontainbleau with M. and Mlle Mallarmé in their little carriage. It was quite uncomfortable with four people in it and the back seat where Mlle Mallarmé and I were sitting kept slipping off.

Julie goes on to describe the château and its salons and apartments, furnishings, tapestries, and decorations in great detail, being especially impressed by the council chamber decorated by Boucher and van Loo with cameos in blue and pink on panels and paintings on the ceiling representing Love, which she found particularly delightful.

Sunday 3rd September

This morning we went into the countryside, but the weather was horrid and gloomy. In the afternoon we stayed at the inn painting and I did the Valvins bridge and the fireworks from memory. We next went to see M. Mallarmé in his study, which is decorated with rush matting and Japanese things, as well as brown material with roses on it.

As we wanted to send a basket of grapes to my godfather [Julie's Oncle-Parrain, the magistrate Maître Jules Dejouy, a cousin of her mother's], Madame Mallarmé took us to see a countrywoman, Mme Badet, who told us to come back tomorrow so that we could watch the grapes being picked.

Monday 4th September

This morning we went to paint watercolours of the Cassepot rocks and I was able to use red lead to show the burnt trees. We packed our case before lunch and afterwards went to M. Mallarmé's, then to Mme Badet's. Her grapes were very good. Monsieur and Mme Mallarmé came with us as far as the inn and stayed with us until our departure in a carriage with a horse which looked like a skeleton. We took an express train and arrived in Paris quite quickly. In a carriage on our way home we went past a lovely old house on the *quai*. We arrived in time for dinner. Octavie was very pleased to see us, but Laërtes didn't even deign to say hello to her.

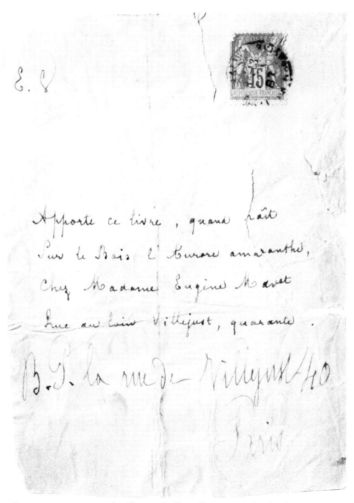

A quatrain on a wrapper on the 'Revue Indépendante' sent by Mallarmé to Berthe Morisot

Madame Edouard Manet, née Suzanne Leenhoff. Julie's Tante Suzanne was a pianist of some note and by all accounts a formidable woman

Thursday 7th September

We went to see Tante Suzanne [Edouard Manet's widow, Suzanne Leenhoff] at Gennevilliers. I liked her much better this time. I took Laërtes along so he could become better acquainted with Follette, who is even uglier than I thought. We didn't stay at Tante Suzanne's for long, as we had come by carriage and were going home the same way. After getting back from Gennevilliers, we set off for the Bois with our coloured crayons. [Julie had been given a new box of crayons for Christmas the previous year.] At the entrance to the Bois, we met my godfather in a carriage. We started by drawing people who were going by on the road around the lake while we were on a lawn right beside the road, on the Pré-Catelan side. Maman and I were sitting very close to each other, with her bag between us on the ground and Laërtes in front. All of a sudden a man in black with a horrible yellow face came towards us, stroked Laërtes, then with a hideous hand seized the bag and fled, running, in the direction of the Pré-Catelan. We screamed. Maman had thrown her penknife and gloves at him straight away without even thinking. Needless to say there was no one about at the time.

I ran off to tell the first person I could find, who happened to be a man from the restaurant who was watering plants. He nodded stupidly and said, 'Oh, really?'

In Maman's bag there was a purse with only 6 francs 50 in it, but what was much more annoying is that we lost the bunch of keys with both door keys, the keys of the secretaire where the silver is kept, and the desk key where the money and jewellery are kept. We were utterly shaken by the experience—apparently I was as white as a sheet and could feel myself trembling. Maman spoke to a park-keeper who was at the top of the lake. He began by saying that the place where we were was not his responsibility, but he took our address and we described the thief to him. When we got home Maman told the police about it, and a person overhearing the story said to Maman, 'I bet you knew him'.

Friday 8th September

This morning I sat for Maman, who is doing my portrait. In the afternoon we went to Durand-Ruel's where there were quite a lot of pictures hanging, all of which I had seen before except three by Puvis de Chavannes.

Having learnt that M. Renoir was in Paris, we climbed all the way up to Montmartre where his house is. There was a spectacular view from there. Since M. and Mme Renoir were out, we were entertained in the garden by Pierre. He wanted to show us his father's paintings and said that they now had two studios, one a bit lower down in Montmartre, and one at home for when M. Renoir had a cold.

After a while Mme Renoir came home. She took us up to the studio and showed us the landscapes M. Renoir did in Brittany. At first sight they produce rather an odd effect; they always have masses of sunshine and trees done with crimson lake, emerald green, and antimony yellow. As one looks at them, however, one begins to find them rather lovely.

Monsieur Renoir got back late and escorted us as far as the foot of Montmartre. It was already after seven; we had stayed there more than two hours. He is supposed to be coming for dinner tomorrow.

Saturday 9th September

Maman worked on my portrait a good part of the morning. In the afternoon we went to Suresnes by boat, to M. Fermé's. The Seine was very pretty; so was Saint-Cloud, which could be seen clearly with its steeple. We came back on foot through the Bois where there were newly-weds everywhere, which was most amusing. All these rather ordinary people seemed to be thrilled to bits to be in a carriage in the Bois de Boulogne for the one and only time in their lives.

We rested not far from the Longchamp racecourse painted so well by Oncle Edouard, with Saint-Cloud in the distance. While we were there we saw Dr Evans, who still seems to be very friendly. Three English Quaker ladies went by in a fiacre, all of them very ugly with their huge black veils. There was something frightening, almost apparition-like about them. Returning along the Avenue des Acacias we saw the little that is left of elegant Parisian society.

Renoir's atelier in Montmartre, called 'Le Château des Brouillards'

Berthe Morisot
Self-portrait with Julie

Monsieur Renoir arrived very late for dinner, appearing with a portrait of Wagner under his arm. He was on his way back from Mme Bonnière's and had got lost in the avenues around Les Invalides. He was carrying Wagner's portrait because a gentleman had asked him for a copy of it, but he didn't know how to go about it. After dinner we looked at the portrait, which is really very handsome. Maman talked about Valvins with M. Renoir, who said that he would come if we went back again—that is, if we are not invited to the Limousin. He himself was once almost invited to go the Limousin by M. Haviland (Mlle Burty's husband).

Monsieur Renoir isn't particularly inspired by Delacroix's *Journal* either.

Pierre Auguste Renoir *Portrait of Richard Wagner. Renoir travelled to Venice in 1882 enjoying the sights and painting the Grand Canal. He then visited Sicily and met Wagner in Palermo. Wagner was 69, in bad health and irritable, but he sat for Renoir for twenty minutes on 15 January, the day he finished 'Parsifal'*

Monday 25th September

Really lovely walk in the forest of ash trees to a clearing which M. Mallarmé calls the 'Ballroom', where he says he will one day hold his daughter's wedding. The huge light-coloured trunks rise up from the ground, which is all russet from the dead leaves.

Julie's cousins, Jeanne and Blanche Pontillon and their brother Edme

Saturday 7th October

Jeanne and Blanche [the Pontillon cousins] had lunch at our house and during the day I went for a walk with them. They seem to find coming back to Paris rather miserable. They are living in the Rue Mignard. After dinner I groomed Laërtes' coat.

Friday 13th October

This morning Maman worked on the portrait of me playing the violin and I sat for two hours.

After lunch we went to fetch Paule and Jeannie [cousins, daughters of Yves Morisot and Théodore Gobillard] to spend the day with us and have dinner. Eugénie [their maid] is also coming for dinner with Octavie, bringing the fish which she is going to cook. Jeannie and I have been copying the portrait of Bon Papa and Bonne Maman [Julie's Manet grandparents] by Oncle Edouard. I started mine in the spring, but it's not making much progress. Jeannie is reading the life of Villiers de l'Isle-Adam. She has read some quite amusing passages from it to me.

Berthe Morisot *Julie and her cousin Jeannie practising*

Wednesday 18th October

Played the violin with Blanche and Jeannie; it was pretty awful. Blanche plays well but lacks breadth in her style. I have done absolutely nothing so far today—it seems to me that the days are too short. I am making a resolution to get up earlier tomorrow, to work, and to be nice to Maman. I plan to practise the violin more, play lots of scales, and learn to play with more gusto.

Friday 20th October

Monsieur, Mme Renoir and Pierre came to lunch so they could see the Russians go past on the Avenue du Bois. We had to wait a very long time for them, and they weren't especially interesting when they did arrive. We didn't have lunch until half past one. There wasn't a huge crowd on the avenue. A few labourers in white shirts had climbed up on ladders, and looked like statues. There were some sort of old barrows for hire and their owners were shouting 'One franc for a place in my elegant carriage'. People were not generally raising the cry *'Vive la Russie'* much. As it was gone half past two by the time we got up from table, we just had a cup of hot chocolate in the evening and went to bed quite early.

Sunday 22nd October

Today I went with Paule, Jeannie and Marcel to the funeral of Maréchal MacMahon. We arrived a bit late, but despite that we were able to find seats on some planks which had been put across packing cases so that we could see the whole parade ground of the Invalides where the troops were marching past MacMahon's body, while the Gardes de Paris prevented the crowds from breaking ranks and from time to time charged on them.

The ceremony was very beautiful. The Napoleon Gate was decorated with black drapery and a simple silver fringe, with the Maréchal's weapon and flags all round. The railings in front also had flags on them and right next to them was the body of the Maréchal MacMahon covered with a great black flag. Général Lancier in front, mounted on a fine horse, watched the troops march past and could be seen from afar with his helmet decorated with white feathers.

The crowd on ladders and planks had only one desire—to see the Russians. They were mistaking the French for Russians. When they came back a few urchins shouted 'Long live the Russians'. Then lots of husbands lifted up their wives so they could see them. The magistrates in red robes and in black robes paraded slowly by. We were able to see the wreaths, the ones from the French were made from roses, dahlias, heliotropes, marguerites and carnations. The one from the Queen of England was pretty, made of Parma violets.

The Maréchal had a funeral worthy of himself. I hadn't seen such an impressive ceremony before. The sarcophagus, which was fairly simple, was pulled by six horses wearing black plumes on their heads. The gas-lamps, which were lit and covered with crêpe, looked very smart. The day was fine, the sun warm.

Monday 30th October

We left early this morning for Giverny. It rained all day. Monsieur Monet showed us his 'cathedrals'. There are twenty-six of them: they're magnificant, some all violet, others white, yellow with a blue sky, pink with a greenish sky; then one in the fog, two or three in shadow at the bottom and lit with rays of sunshine on the towers. These cathedrals, admirably drawn, are painted in broad areas, and yet one can see every detail. They're so confusing. It seems so hard to me not to draw all the details. These pictures by M. Monet are an excellent lesson in painting. The house has changed since the last time we went to Giverny. Monsieur Monet has made himself a bedroom above the studio, with big windows, doors and a floor in pitchpine, decorated in white. In this room lots of paintings are hung, among them: Isabelle combing her hair, Gabrielle at the basin, Cocotte with a hat on, a pastel of Maman's, a pastel by Oncle Edouard, a very attractive nude by M. Renoir, some Pissarros, etc.

Claude Monet in his 'studio' at Giverny, where he never painted but in which he hung a large number of his own works reflecting the different periods and tendencies of his art

A shady walk in Monet's garden at Giverny

Madame Monet's bedroom has blue panelling, those of Mlles Blanche and Germaine are mauve. We didn't see Mlle Marthe's bedroom. Mademoiselle Blanche showed us some of her own paintings, which are a lovely colour, two of them of trees reflected in the Epte are very like M. Monet's painting.

The drawing-room is panelled in violet—lots of Japanese prints are hung there as well as in the dining-room, which is all yellow. We walked beneath the poplars to see the greenhouse where there are magnificent crysanthemums. Then on to the ornamental lake across which is a green bridge which looks rather Japanese. Monsieur and Mme Butler came—their little boy is sweet; he kept on trying to pull my hair (he's six months old).

We came home before dinner, still in the pouring rain, on the new line from Mantes to Argenteuil. I could just see the trees and roof of Le Mesnil in the darkness. I think it's quite delightful to have a château one doesn't even live in, and to be able from time to time to see it from a train, appearing like a shadow in the night, and to say to oneself 'It's mine'.

1893

Wednesday 1st November

All Saints' Day, a sad day. A year ago we were at Tours and in '91 we still had Papa with us. How sad it is to lose a father, especially when one still lives at home, and never to see him again, never ever. Often, when I dream about Papa, I feel so unhappy when I wake up. I really need him. I want to see him, to hear him, to speak to him, and be nice to him. Why can't I be nicer to Maman? Every day I chide myself about this, but don't do enough about it.

Thursday 2nd November

Maman, Paule, Jeannie and I went to St Germain this morning to hear a sung mass for the dead; it was extremely beautiful: religious ceremonies are magnificent with those lovely voices which seem to float above the altar.

Sunday 5th November

Went to one of the Concerts Colonne today—Maman, Jeannie, and I. We walked back along the *quais*. The day was drawing to a close with a few gas-lamps alight; the old part of Paris, still as attractive as ever, with towers rising up near the Seine, was delightful.

Maman and I went to see my Oncle Parrain this morning. We hadn't seen him since the arrival of the Russians. He still looks all right [Julie's godfather had had a stroke].

Thursday 9th November

Paule, Jeannie and Marcel [their brother] came to dinner. We talked about Mlle Bashkirtseff and how she used to write to all the well-known people. She even asked Alexandre Dumas to meet her at a rendezvous she had chosen. Our conversation came round to Jacques-Emile Blanche, who has given Maman absolutely no sign of life for some time; then on to M. de Wyzewa, who last year rented a country house and was then obliged to leave it, saying it was haunted. He never comes to visit us. We said goodbye to Marcel who is off to Commercy on Saturday to do his military service. This year is a hard one for him.

Friday 10th November

Maman and I went to the Louvre—it was rather a gloomy day. We admired a Jordaens, THE CHILDHOOD OF JUPITER, which has recently been lowered. Then our eyes fell on a portrait by van Loo of a father with his little boy, which is beautiful. In the Salon Carré a little Japanese man was copying a Leonardo da Vinci, but in a completely Japanese style. It was most amusing.

Next we visited my Oncle Parrain; then went on to the Rudy Institute to see about French classes. The young lady who gives them is very pleasant. They're held twice a week, Tuesday and Thursday, from two to four. We are to start on Tuesday. The piano lessons which Jeannie might be going to are also on Tuesdays at the same time so we would be able to travel together, which would be a help.

Berthe Morisot *Julie's father, Eugène Manet, with Julie in the garden at Bougival. The rented villa at 4 Rue de la Princesse was the family's summer residence from 1881 until 1885 when they made their permanent home at 40 Rue de Villejust*

1894

Julie's godfather dies
A trip to Brussels with Berthe Morisot
The Libre Esthétique—Paris again
The Duret Collection—Death of Tzar Alexander III
A visit to the dealer Camentron
At Tante Suzanne's—Julie's sixteenth birthday
A night at the Comédie Française

Edouard Manet *'Le Bouquet de Violettes': portrait of Berthe Morisot painted in 1872*

1894

Friday 9th March

This morning my poor Oncle Parrain died. It is just two years since he fell ill. How tragic it is to see all one's family dying like this . . . first Papa, then my Aunt Yves, and now my godfather.

Monday 12th March

Today it was the funeral of my Oncle Parrain at the Madeleine; tomorrow he will be buried at Gennevilliers. Maman went to the house, but I only went to the church with Paule. It's the first time I've been to a funeral. How sad to think that I'll never again see him, or any of the others who are dead. Paule gave me a very affectionate kiss as we went out. She is well acquainted with grief. Poor Paule and Jeannie are orphans and all alone in life. Their brother doesn't give them much support.

Tuesday 13th March

Today my godfather was buried at Gennevilliers. Maman was there for a very long time. In the evening we left for Brussels and stayed at the Hôtel de Suède, which Tante Suzanne mentioned, whose proprietor [Henri Van Cutsem] is also the owner of ARGENTEUIL by Oncle Edouard.

Wednesday 14th March

Went sightseeing all morning. The cathedral of Ste Gudule is gorgeous. Set in a square with a slight slope, it has great staircases; and the delicate arches look as though made of marble. Magnificent old stained-glass windows in beautiful colours are in one of the chapels.

We went through the Place de l'Hôtel de Ville which is very handsome; opposite is the king's house, which is gilded as are other buildings around the square. It certainly gives the impression of great wealth.

Got back very late for lunch and then went out again to buy thick woollens as it's very cold here. Dinner at the hotel at six, not many guests there. I was glad to get to bed after writing to Jeannie as I am finding the trip tiring.

Julie's beloved 'Oncle Parrain', Maître Jules Dejouy, who was of the Manet family

Thursday 15th March

In the morning, visited M. Van Cutsem's collection, but about the only attractive picture was Oncle Edouard's. The rest are Belgian painters, among whom is a M. Collin who asked us to visit and who was well pleased with his own work (really pretty awful, if the truth be known).

Went to the Libre Esthétique where Maman has exhibited. It's very well set out. All sorts of things are there to be seen: paintings, pewter, embroidery, tapestry, books and furniture. From the window one can see all Brussels, with its town hall, of which the splendid belfry rises among the rooftops.

As for paintings, there are lots of things, both the Pissarros (father and son), the water-colours of one of them are very pretty; some Denis, Gauguin etc. . . . I am forgetting a lovely thing by M. Renoir—two tiny women reading the same book, one in pink, the other in green, both full length. This canvas is to be found in the same gallery as Maman's paintings, which look very good too.

Friday 16th March

We took the train back in the evening, having dinner in the dining-car. At the border we went into the first-class carriage, where we got some sleep. Finally we arrived home in Paris, at Rue Weber by 11 o'clock, and went to bed.

Saturday 17th March

Paule and Jeannie came to see us this morning. During the day there was an exhibition of the Duret Collection before the sale, which was lovely. The collection consists of one of Maman's paintings of a woman dressed in a low-cut white robe on which is a garland of glorious white flowers; several of Oncle Edouard's large canvases: LE REPOS (a portrait of Maman dressed in white on a red sofa with one foot stretched out in front), LE PÈRE LATHUILE, and a small portrait of Maman in three-quarter profile, dressed in black with a bouquet of violets and wearing a small hat. I adore this portrait—the brushwork is so good and the blacks are quite magnificent, as are the whites in the other portrait. What wonderful brushwork Oncle Edouard had.

There is also a very attractive picture by M. Monet in the collection, of some white turkeys on a great lawn and behind them a castle made of brick, surrounded by pine trees, and a forest beyond. As for M. Renoir's two paintings, they're really lovely—one landscape and one of a nude combing her hair. There is a certain grace in this one; the head, which is slightly foreshortened, is delightful, and the whole picture is in very attractive, pleasant colours.

The one painter who I like very much, from what I have seen of his here, is Cézanne; above all it's his well-modelled apples that I like (I only know these three paintings by him). I was forgetting a painting of Albert Wolff by Oncle Edouard (unfinished), a wonderful portrait, such as only Manet could have painted, and it must be an extremely good likeness. Looking at this portrait one has to say: what a marvellous thing—especially considering how stupid and ugly the sitter is. Also in the collection are some of M. Degas' racehorses and some of the beautifully drawn dancers of this great master.

Friday 2nd November

We took a car to go to the cemetery at Gennevilliers where the body of my poor godfather is buried, and put a wreath and a bouquet on his tomb. My dear old Oncle Parrain, the last of the Manets. Now I really am the only descendant of the three Manet brothers; there remain only one unhappy young girl and two widows to mourn them. We went on to Tante Suzanne's where we saw some albums of drawings which Oncle Edouard did on his journeys—they're rough pen-drawings of sculptures, paintings etc. We brought back three of them—a red chalk drawing of a woman after Raphael, I think, and two water-colour medallions, one of the Three Graces on a mauve ground, the other a woman with a violin at her side, probably Ste Cecilia.

The Tzar [Alexander III] who has been very ill for many days has died at Livadia. When he arrived there, someone remarked to him that it was funny to have named a sea so blue the Black Sea. 'If it has been named the Black Sea', he said, 'it's because it's going to see me die.' Unfortunately it was true.

Monsieur Renoir called while we were having our literature lesson with M. Mauclair. The latter spoke about secret writing in French, *écriture secrète*, but had nothing of particular interest to say.

Quatrain by Mallarmé addressed to Berthe Morisot and Julie in Brittany—summer 1894

Wednesday 7th November

Went to M. Camentron's. As always he is sure he can sell some of Maman's paintings; but they've been there for a year now. He had a beautiful pastel of a woman at a dressmaker's trying on a hat in front of a cheval-mirror by Degas. Racehorses and dancers too. And he showed us a photograph of a piece of the first sketch of L'EXÉCUTION DE MAXIMILIEN. This painting was at the printing works of Tante Suzanne's brother, M. Léon [Leenhoff], who firstly cut out the figure of Maximilien to sell it separately, then the rest passed to M. Camentron and M. Portier; it was the latter who cut off the sergeant behind the soldiers. This means the painting is now in three sections. Monsieur Degas is looking for them, and has already found two. He's going to reassemble them and try to put the painting back as it was.

On Thursday, when we went to Tante Suzanne's, Maman rightly asked her what had become of this sketch. 'It is absolutely ruined', she replied, 'it was so damp in Léon's printing works, it wasn't worth anything.'

We went to see Mme Jammes, who was very pleasant, she knows Paimpol and the Île Bréhat, and likes Britanny and the Breton people.

I might have to go to history classes which start on Thursday 15th, and most certainly to the science classes which begin on Saturday 17th.

Wednesday 14th November

It's my sixteenth birthday. The sunrise was quite extraordinary—it was magical, pink, pink everywhere like a Bengal flare, everything looked as though it was enveloped in tarlatan—marvellous. Paule and Jeannie brought me flowers and Berthe [Renault] sent some lovely plants. We went to Mme Renault for dinner and afterwards to the Français [Comédie Française]. First we heard Molière's *Mariage Forcé*; this parody has some quite amusing moments; the calm philosopher is entertaining, while the other one is vulgar.

Julie Manet aged 16 years

40

DANS CETTE MAISON
CONSTRUITE ET HABITEE
PAR BERTHE MORISOT
1841 - 1895
VECUT ET MOURUT
PAUL VALERY
1871 - 1945

1895

The plaque outside 40 Rue Paul Valéry, formerly Rue de Villejust, commemorating Berthe Morisot and Paul Valéry. The house was built for Berthe Morisot and her husband and subsequently occupied by Julie and her Gobillard cousins, one of whom—Jeannie—married Paul Valéry. The street was renamed in 1945

1895

Friday 1st March

Maman has been very ill since I last wrote anything. The doctor thinks she has pulmonary congestion and comes twice a day, yet says that the illness is following its natural course and that he finds Maman somewhat better today. She is terribly weak, can scarcely speak, takes only a little milk, but the fever isn't very strong. She is suffering a great deal with her throat, which prevents her from swallowing. She was extremely ill last evening and today about 4 o'clock. Tante Edma spent last night at her bedside and is doing the same tonight. Paule is staying all day, Blanche takes me out walking, and lots of people come for news of Maman.

I am surrounded by affectionate people who are taking good care of Maman and we are pleased with the doctor. I would do absolutely anything to get Maman better quickly, it gives me so much pain to see her ill like this. It's hard not to cry. And if only I could do something useful—I don't know how to nurse and everyone wants me to go to sleep at night. How bleak this all is. Dear God, make Maman better.

Wednesday 17th April

Oh, sorrow! since I last wrote I have lost Maman. She died at half past ten on Saturday 2nd March. I cannot describe the enormity of my grief, the depth of my sadness. In three years my parents have left me and now I am an orphan.

Poor Maman, she suffered so much to have to leave me; she saw the end coming and didn't want me to go into her room to have such a sad memory of her. Her illness was short but painful; the sore throat was frightful and she could no longer breathe. Oh! never, never would I have believed that such a terrible thing could happen. On Saturday morning she was still laughing; she was able to see my cousin Gabriel; how pretty she was then; she was her usual self; she was fine.

At 3 o'clock I spoke to Maman for the last time. At seven Dr Ganne came, I went into Maman's room, but it was impossible to stay—I couldn't bear to see her suffering like that, unable to breathe. I could see her dying and I thought she would be cured. I thought we had already had enough misfortune. About 10 o'clock Dr Ganne came back accompanied by a short doctor in evening dress, whom I only saw for a second and who will remain for ever in my mind as a figure from a nightmare. (Oh! if only it were just a nightmare.) But, no, alas, it's reality.

Oh God! help me to bear this loss, sustain me, you alone can help us in our adversity, and, if I've lived thus far, it's only through your grace. Yes, dear God, you are infinitely good; make Maman happy at your side.

The ground-floor drawing-room in Berthe Morisot's house in the Rue de Villejust as it is at the present time and much as it used to be at the beginning of the century. Over the bureau, on which stand the wax and bronze heads of Julie by her mother dated 1887, is Manet's portrait of Berthe Morisot

One of the last-known photographs of Berthe Morisot, c. 1894

There was a profound silence in the room, then voices—I was listening from the dining-room. I was taken to the landing on the staircase, where I remained with Blanche and Jeannie, trembling. I heard a cry (it was Marie [the maid], who had fainted from the awful thing that had just happened).

Suddenly Julies changes tense and relives the last moments of her mother's life.

The doctors come out. Someone takes me to my room. Blanche tells me that things are going badly and I cannot see Maman. Blanche comes back, puts me to bed, stays beside my bed. Ah! if she can stay, then it must mean that it's all over. I fall asleep having understood and yet not believing it all the same. I hope for an awakening when I will find Maman better. Oh! When I look back over all the agonies of this day, I feel as if my heart is going to break.

Oh! my dearest Maman—she left a letter for me, a letter which is so precious; and she wrote to Jeannie: 'I leave Julie in your care.' Her last word was Julie. How much she went through for me. The night of Friday to Saturday was dreadful, but Maman said she wanted to stay alive until the morning so she could see me again. During the night Marie went to find a homoeopath, who came in the morning. Maman wanted one. Oh, misery!, never did I think I would be without Maman.

My dearest little Julie, I love you as I die; I will still love you when I am dead; I beg of you, do not cry; this parting was inevitable. I would have liked to be with you until you married . . . Work hard and be good as you always have been; you have never caused me one sorrow in your little life. You have beauty, money; make good use of them. I think the best thing would be to live with your cousins in the Rue de Villejust, but I do not wish to force you to do anything. Give your Tante Edma a remembrance of me, and your cousins too; and give Monet's BATEAUX EN RÉPARATION to your cousin Gabriel [Gabriel Thomas]. Tell M. Degas that if he founds a museum he is to choose a Manet. A keepsake for Monet; one for Renoir; and one of my drawings for Bartholomé. Give something to the two concierges. Do not cry. I love you more than I can tell you. Jeannie, I leave Julie in your care.

After her mother's death Julie did in fact go back to live at 40 Rue de Villejust, where she shared an apartment with two of her cousins, Jeannie and Paule (who was considerably older than her sister and Julie).
That summer Julie spent a holiday in Brittany with M. and Mme Renoir.

Renoir in Brittany

Thursday 8th August

We [Julie, Jeannie, and Paule] left Dinard in the morning. We were going to meet M. Renoir at Châteaulin. We changed trains first at Dinan, then at Lamballe, and again at St Brieuc. Next we took a train to Landerneau. There, after having changed for the last time, we heard a man shouting. He was being carried into the next compartment by some Breton men. Into ours came a man with a red nose and a rough voice saying that it was a madman who was being mistreated, that those looking after him had an enormous barrel of fine wine [*une barrique*: a 225-litre barrel of wine] which they were drinking, and not giving any to the madman and so on and so forth.

The train left; the traveller opened a suitcase; the smell of wine escaped; and we saw one full bottle, another broken, and the wine was running all over the carriage. He then offered us pears and plums, saying: 'Accept these from an old sea-wolf.' We were rather frightened though a military man reassured us. Then he pulled out a bottle of spirits and started drinking, so at the very first station, where the train only stopped for one minute, we grabbed our things and jumped out of the second-class carriage and got into the first class, not sorry to have left this man who seemed to be fairly drunk. We were anxious to find M. Renoir. Thankfully we saw him at Châteaulin station and he took us to an hotel, where we spent the night.

Saturday 10th August

We left at six in the morning for Douarnenez, where we were fired with enthusiasm for the bay despite the frightful grey, harsh weather. A few trees and some thatched roofs had broken loose into the sea and the coastline, which is an enchanting shape, surrounded and enclosed the infinity of the ocean. Below us sailing boats, one after another, made an imperceptible dark blurr in the distance.

Douarnenez itself is dirty and the population has an unhealthy air. Monsieur Renoir remained in order to visit a house in the area while we went back to Quimper for lunch. We visited the cathedral, which we admired both inside and out. Then we walked about among the narrow streets with their beamed or slate-roofed houses—and always above the roofs can be seen the delicate, high-pointed towers of the magnificent cathedral, built in a very fine style, which is similar to that of Chartres (or so M. Renoir tells us).

In the middle of the afternoon we met M. Renoir at the station; he had found a very nice little house at Tréboul, near Douarnenez. We headed in the direction of Pont-Aven, got out at Bannelec, and there took a bus for Pont-Aven. Pierre had come to meet us and we found Mme Renoir with Jean and his nursemaid at the entrance to the Hôtel des Voyageurs. The neighbourhood seemed quite pretty.

We were served at table by delightful maids who wear big pleated muslin collars and a bonnet with ribbons which goes underneath the Pont-Aven *coiffe* with its huge bows.

Sunday 11th August

At mass all the women in their bonnets looked immaculate; and the men, standing against the pillars, were handsome in their high embroidered collars. The person who took the collection had long grey hair combed forward.

Pierre Auguste Renoir aged about 50

Thursday 15th August

For this feast day [the Assumption] the Breton people wore their most beautiful costumes. Our dresses seemed very shabby beside the silk aprons of every colour, the embroidered velvets, the ribbons in pink, blue, violet, green etc., beneath the white *coiffes* and the collars bordered with lace. Julia, one of the maids from the hotel, a ravishing brunette with a handsome face, who seems to be quite a flirt but kind too, had a beautiful collar bordered with huge daisies embroidered by hand.

During the day we watched the procession which was forming on the quay and the varnishing of the boats. Some of the little girls had white dresses and one woman wore a dress completely covered in gold embroidery.

The procession over, we went off for a walk with M. Renoir. He took us to the Château de Ruste, which is in ruins and where one can see ghosts, so it's said—a monk and a lady in white, who appear on a certain night each month. Then we went on to Nizon, which was quite pretty, and had a good church and a calvary.

Friday 16th August

Paule wasn't well, so Jeannie stayed with her and I went with M. and Mme Renoir to the beach at St Nicholas, which is at the entrance to the Aven. We went there by boat in the morning and came back only just in time for dinner, passing two châteaux, and Rosbras, where Maman, Tante Yves, and Tante Edma once lived. I could see their house, which is now surrounded by fir trees. We saw this countryside, which our mothers told us about so often, but sadly without them.

We bathed before lunch. In this primitive part of the country one has to undress outdoors behind a rock, and eat on the ground as best one can. Monsieur Renoir did a delightful study under the trees; one could see in it all the richness of the colours of the shadows beneath the trees on a very hot day and in the background the intensely blue sea glittering. Jean had lots of fun in the water—he's very sweet with his golden hair.

Friday 23rd August

This morning we painted in the woods below Pont-Aven. We went by carriage to Quimperlé for the day, arriving in the town via a square planted with trees and surrounded by water from where one had a view of the houses crowded around the church with its square belfry. First of all we visited this round church built on the model of the great mosque at Constantinople. It was curious; there were many altars at different levels, one of them seemed to be in a cellar, two others were at ground level, and another was above, to which one climbed up, like getting on to a bridge.

Next we searched in the Rue du Château (where there is a ruined church) for the house of M. de Lassalle, a relative and neighbour of my Tante Chevalier; we found it and M. de Lassalle, who I didn't know, opened the door to us, looked at us with an air of astonishment, then cried: 'Good gracious! the young Morisot ladies!' He asked us into a small parlour where two old Quimperlé ladies, mother and daughter, were sitting, dressed in the style of fifty years ago. They talked to us about our mothers who once stayed in this town. Tante Yves lived here, and when we went out with our old cousin he showed us the house where Paule was born, in the square, a lovely riverside house, with roses around the door.

Later we crossed some ancient lanes, passed two timbered houses with jutting first storeys and climbed up to the old church, which, situated in the square where the market is held, had a fine porch. Inside, beneath some old gilded statues (including quite a funny one of the Virgin Mary), the Way of the Cross was in pretty colours. In front of the altar, a man who'd had too much to drink (which seems to happen rather often with the Bretons) was asleep with a staff by his side. After we had looked round Quimperlé, which we liked very much, M. de Lassalle gave us such a big tea that when we got back to the hotel in Pont-Aven we could only manage a hot drink. There a discussion on Oncle Edouard took place between M. Renoir and an ill-informed amateur painter, M. Hérart. He said that he didn't admire everything about Manet. Renoir replied that in that case M. Hérart didn't really like Manet; that when one admired the work of a master there could be nothing displeasing in it at all. Monsieur Hérart kept on about Delaunay, whose painting he liked so much. He had painted his mother's portrait, so beautifully that it had all crackled. 'That proves that it's a bad picture', said M. Renoir. 'Painting is a craft which must be learnt; a good picture is well painted.'

After a few jokes from M. Hérart in which he said that the answer must be to be a painter and decorator, M. Renoir said that he was still learning his craft, that he wanted always to learn more and never be content with what he was doing. 'I have a great deal of ambition', he said. 'I would rather not paint at all than be a mediocre painter.' Monsieur Hérart, over-excited, ended up by saying that OLYMPIA was atrocious and he repeated this endlessly. Monsieur Renoir almost lost his temper and the discussion was interminable.

It always provokes me when someone attacks my uncle's work like this, and, even though I tell myself that anyone who says his paintings are monstrosities must be an imbecile, I still want to reply, and I get angry.

Saturday 24th August

I woke up with a crick in my neck and spent the day in our bedroom. In the evening M. Renoir showed us what he had been doing at Pont-Aven. Then he told us the story about the time he didn't know if Catulle Mendès lived in the Rue de Trévise or in the Cité de Trévise. Monsieur Renoir was only able to recognize Mendès' house because he had Japanese curtains hung at the windows of the second floor. On one occasion, wearing evening dress, M. Renoir saw these curtains at the windows of a house in the Rue de Trévise, so he went up the stairs and rang the bell. A maid opened the door, but he was astonished when he realized the interior was not that of Mendès' apartment. Then he heard voices, people who sounded as though they were getting up and putting on their boots etc., so he rushed through the door and down the stairs two by two, with the maids shouting 'Monsieur! Monsieur!' after him. He was overjoyed to find himself safely back in the street, and knew then, once and for all, that Catulle Mendès must live in the Cité de Trévise. However for that evening, one adventure being quite enough, he went straight home, flabbergasted that there could be two houses exactly the same, both with Japanese curtains on the second floor.

Sunday 25th August

We didn't go out all day. In the evening M. Renoir got involved in a discussion about the war; he took exception to a young man who said he would never take up arms unless it were to defend a personal ideal. What an astonishing concept, and to say so in front of complete strangers, too. A lot of people must share the same idea if he dares to voice such a shocking opinion.

Julie Manet *View of l'Ile de Noirmoutier, where the Rouart family still spend their holidays*

Saturday 14th September

Jeannie and I went off to paint on the clifftop at Tréboul this morning. The sea was a soft blue, and the coastline rose-coloured; Île Tristan was clearly visible and Douarnenez was silhouetted against the clear sky and the sun which whitened everything and was reflected in the water. The mountain [*sic*] behind was all blue and over this delightful landscape with its beautiful colours floated the morning mist, softening the strong tones. A number of boats, with sails which had become grey with age, went by and formed a lilac-coloured mass standing out against the light.

Coming back along the little path on the cliff we remarked upon the delightful sound of the impact of the water at the far end of a miniature grotto. In the water a jelly-fish was floating, taking on hues of yellow, green, pink, lilac.

At the end of the day we went to fetch M. Renoir at the farm. We walked with him to the white rocks from where one can see the entrance to the bay. There, as we watched the sunset, the gorse covered heaths turned first gold then russet; the sun, in its splendour, encircled by crimson and purple, made a great luminous trail in the water and a rose-coloured glimmer spread everywhere. On the way back we could see the coastline and the mountain plunged into a soft blue-grey.

Thursday 19th September

Madame Renoir told us about her trip to Italy after her marriage. We found it quite funny to hear her telling us all this, because we'd so often heard M. Renoir talk about it as though he had made the trip on his own, back in the days when we didn't even know his wife.

She was twenty-two and was very slim, she said (which is hard to believe). She also told us that the first time she saw M. Renoir he was with M. Monet and Sisley; all three wore their hair long and they caused quite a stir when they walked along the Rue St Georges where she lived.

When he was young M. Renoir spent his summers painting in the Forest of Fontainebleau [at Barbizon]. He had a place to stay at 50 sous a day, and Diaz who was with him at the time used to sell his paintings as Rousseau's. He did about eight of them a day. The result is that now lots of Renoirs are taken for Rousseaus. How I'd love to see them.

After a swim and a lovely walk around Tréboul we climbed up near the Moulins from where the view over Douarnenez lit by the last rays of the sun was very attractive.

Sunday 22nd September

I've been bathing all week—we are absolutely mad on swimming. I can float now and turn over in the water but I would like to be able to dive and really swim properly.

It's extremely agreeable to get into the sea, surrounded by this beautiful coastline after having had the sun on one's back all morning, painting. It's an arduous trade, being a landscape painter, but there are other harder ones, I think, such as being a fisherman.

Before dinner we went to to see the fishermen preparing for their departure, for on Sundays they have the day off. The boats are in harbour and the sailors go drinking; in the evening they go back to their boats, a little unsteady on their feet, with their bags on their backs. The women wear clean clothes, the children are on the quay.

This evening the sky, which was all pink with light lilac clouds, was reflected in the water and the boats stood out in black beneath.

We came back by a road which runs along the cliff and stopped to watch night falling, the trees in the cemetery, and the crosses on the tombs etched against the silver sea where two black sails, made larger by their own reflections, were passing by.

Tuesday 24th September

Jeannie and I went for a nice walk with M. Renoir and Pierre. The weather was dull. It was the sort of morning when one has a rest from painting in order to get to know the area, carrying an umbrella instead of a paintbox. We went across country, taking the tiny Audièrne railway. We had intended to go as far as Poulan but stopped at a superb pine forest where the sound of the wind played an enchanting symphony.

From the road, bordered with excellent mulberry trees, gorse and heather, one could see the heath-land above and a few pine trees behind immersed in a light mist, Douarnenez and its mountain taking on an extraordinary grandeur.

Then, through an empty space in the flowering furze, a patch of sea could be seen, with the coastline like a firm blue rule forming the horizon. The whole effect is at once grandiose, desolate, and pleasant—there is something of the Midi here. The landscape made M. Renoir think of Italy and the studies of Old Father Corot, as he calls him. He often speaks of him as being the greatest landscapist; indeed there are some simply marvellous things by him. Here, in this land of Finistère which I love, this wild countryside, one feels as though one were at the end of the earth, but not in a sad sort of way—it's wonderful!

Thursday 26th September

Worked morning and evening on the cliffs above Tréboul. Monsieur Renoir came to fetch us. He said that I knew how to get houses just right. Such a compliment from a great master gave me pleasure but perhaps it's just vanity? However it does seem to me that one should be able to be pleased when someone who knows tells you, when you have worked very hard, that it's not completely wanting.

Certainly I do have many faults—I want to work hard at everything this year. Unfortunately after the holidays I always feel disposed to do great things; then, little by little, when it gets cold, I get up late, go skating in the middle of the day, have cups of tea, and the day goes by without my having achieved much at all. I don't want it to be like this any more.

1895

Monday 30th September

Jean has been ill since yesterday. Monsieur Renoir went for the doctor. He said he had colic. The poor little mite cries all day—it's sad to hear him.

Quite impossible to work above Tréboul at the end of the day—the boys here are unbearable.

At the beginning of October Julie went back to Paris

Friday 4th October

At four in the morning we had to wait two hours in the station at Tours and didn't arrive in Paris until half past eleven. The journey really was rather too long . . . Monsieur Renoir has been so kind and so charming all summer; the more one sees of him, the more one realizes he is a true artist, first class and extraordinarily intelligent, but also with a genuine simple heartedness.

Paris seemed grey and ugly to us, a deserted and tasteless place. I was seized by a profound sadness on entering the apartment, which breathed loneliness, where every object brought Maman to mind, at the same time reminding me that she is no

The third-floor apartment at the Rue de Villejust, where Julie and her cousins lived after Berthe Morisot's death

Julie Manet *A young Breton girl in traditional head-dress*

Julie Manet *Jeannie Gobillard in a garden. This charming picture shows how much Julie was influenced by Renoir*

Julie Manet *Mallarmé sailing on the Seine near Valvins*

longer here. Away one could make believe one was living in a dream, but here one is certain of not seeing her ever again. It's over, how sad! Not to see you again, Maman, what grief! These beautiful paintings which I look at with such pleasure make me cry.

Saturday 26th October

We spent a day with Berthe [Renault] and we three friends bewailed the fact that the end of the world be in 1900 and France would be destroyed next year (according to Hachette's *Almanach*). We thought it extremely tedious to witness the end of the world, and horrid to see France divided—in other words, war. We hoped it wouldn't actually happen. Then we thought the end of the world was nigh because everybody seemed to be completely crazy. Berthe said: 'In the olden days girls liked the spring, the sun, now they only like autumn, winter, and the moon.'

(Undated)

Monsieur Degas can think of nothing but photography. He has invited us all to have dinner with him next week and he'll take our photograph by artificial light: the only thing is you have pose for three minutes. He wanted to see if we would make good models and made M. Renoir pose, but he started laughing. Paule mentioned M. Mauclair's article and M. Degas flew into a rage saying: 'Oh, critics! they're the ones who give the orders nowadays. They think painting is their domain because they can speak of a certain blue, etc.' (I am not able to repeat his words exactly as they were spoken—it would take the fire out of them otherwise. So I'll stop.)

Monsieur Mallarmé listening to all this seemed very unhappy; M. Renoir was beaming, for his opinion on critics is the same as M. Degas'.

It was decided that we would dine at M. Degas' on Wednesday. 'You will see Zoë, my maid', he told us, 'who has put on weight.'

I don't know why people say he's disagreeable, he has such a nice way about him and kisses us in such a fatherly manner. But then, artists are first rate. Monsieur Renoir is quite touching in the way he looks after us and the way he talks to us about Maman's exhibition for instance. He looked at a portfolio of water-colours which he thought were delightful and he explained what needed to be done to frame these gems, the majority of them almost unknown. What an absolutely charming mother I had (not to be able to say 'have' any more is hard). How virtuous she was. She embodied both the artist and the tender mother. I want to cry when I see these water-colours: a woman in a boat on the lake, with the words 'lady—duck' etc. inscribed on it to teach me to read; a nursemaid, children playing hide and seek, and lots of others; Marcel, Nini, and Bibi [probably the three children of Yves Gobillard; Berthe Morisot's pet name for her daughter was also Bibi] having a meal. Maman had intended to make a whole album like this to teach children how to read, but she didn't put her idea into effect. I regret it very much as it would have been charming.

We agree with M. Renoir that M. Mallarmé will write a very good preface to the catalogue because he more than anyone else can speak about the life of the magnificent woman who was my Maman.

Still on the subject of the Mauclair article, M. Renoir told us that he didn't like the Puvis de Chavannes much; that they seemed to him to be paintings one could pull out and lengthen at will. 'If you want an extra metre we can unroll it for you', he joked; also he says his men are hardly recognizable from his women, and so do I. After dinner M. Renoir told us that M. Zandomeneghi was at loggerheads with him because, although M. Renoir often visited him, as he lived in the same building, he never bothered to return his calls. Monsieur Renoir did a marvellous imitation of him, with his Italian accent, showing him his paintings. Monsieur Renoir, still finding them frightful, said: 'It's very nice, but there's a blue in the background that I think is a bit bright.'

'It's precisely because of that blue' replied M. Zandomeneghi, 'that I did this picture', and promptly took it to Durand-Ruel's. There, all the staff made fun of his blue and he was obliged to go home and cover it up. Monsieur Renoir told us lots of other stories about him, but they wouldn't have the same charm if told other than by M. Renoir with the Italian painter's nasal accent.

Thursday 14th November

I'm seventeen today. Paule made me a Breton cake surrounded by flowers and invited Geneviève to lunch; we had dinner at Berthe's, like last year. I recalled the day when we went to the Français with Maman. Every year I become more unhappy as more and more sad occasions accumulate in my thoughts. A year ago I was relatively happy (if one can be happy after having seen one's father and part of one's family die), but I still had a mother who was always near me and whose side I never left.

Sunday 17th November

Had lunch at M. Renoir's, where we spent a very pleasant day. He showed us the portrait of a model with a ravishing hat of white chiffon with a rose on it (which he had made himself) and wearing a white dress with a green belt. The picture is

Geneviève, only daughter of Stéphane Mallarmé, born in 1864, in the gateway at Valvins, c. 1885

extremely pretty, the clothes light and delicate, and the brown hair very beautiful. And we saw the portrait of Jean with Gabrielle [a favourite model and member of the Renoir household] which is charming.

Wednesday 20th November

Arrived quite late at M. Degas' house. We met Zoë on the stairs and she let us in— M. Mallarmé, M. Renoir and M. Bartholomé were there, and M. Degas was very busy arranging a lamp he had just bought, which gave off a brilliant light. I admired the portrait of my Oncle Edouard by him, which I hadn't seen before.

This portrait was the cause of an argument. Monsieur Degas had painted Tante

Suzanne at the piano and Oncle Edouard lying on a sofa listening; the latter finding that his wife looked too ugly, cut her off. Monsieur Degas quite reasonably became angry with this conduct and took back the canvas, which he now has in his drawing-room. He also has Tante Suzanne on a sofa in pastel and Oncle Edouard's JAMBON.

In his house the paintings are hung up anywhere or simply put on the floor. His dining-room is decorated with yellow hankerchiefs and above are some Ingres drawings. Rumour has it that he always serves the same dinner—*rillettes de pays*, chicken, salad, and preserves, all prepared by Zoë, who serves while making conversation and seems to be a very good soul. 'Zoë, you should make more crust', M. Degas says to her, 'Another time I'll put more on', etc. etc.

The conversation turned to Zandomeneghi. Monsieur Degas is doing his portrait and he only wants to sit for about two hours each week. Everyone remarked on his disagreeable personality.

Talking about Glatigny, M. Mallarmé recounted that he had met this astonishing man at Versailles and that people were giving him rhymes and that he was composing two different poems at the same time. He offered him a drink at some café, but Glatigny replied that he would rather have a pair of socks; so M. Mallarmé took him to buy some. He took off his old ones there and then, put on the new ones, and left, much to the amazement of the shop assistants.

Carolus Duran and Zacharie Astruc were also discussed. They lived together and used to flatter each other, joking: 'How handsome you are, Shakespeare! How handsome you are, Velasquez!' At one of the Salons, each thought he had won a prize and loudly praised his own work. But it was Carolus Duran who was the winner.

Astruc was in the habit of never paying his models, and, while walking past his own front door with someone or other one day, he saw written in chalk: 'I came for my money, Calire or whatever your name is.' He pretended not to see it, and rubbed off the words 'for my money' with his thumb. Monsieur Degas told the story with his usual flair.

We sat for ages around the table and I listened with pleasure to these four great artists talking; yet I thought about our charming Thursday dinners with sadness— it seems so extraordinary not to see Papa and Maman among them all.

Wednesday 27th November

We went to see Tante Suzanne, who now lives in a very nice apartment at Asnières. She is much better off there than in that damp house at Gennevilliers.

Edgar Degas *Portrait of Yves Gobillard, Berthe Morisot's sister*

Friday 29th November

Left to see M. Renoir, whom we met near his studio. 'Do you want to go and see M. Degas?' he asked; so off we went to M. Degas' sudio, where he opened the door himself. 'Why hello, how are you?' he said to me at once. 'I'm sorry, the photographs were all failures, I haven't dared to get in touch with you.'

His studio is very cluttered. He's doing a lot of work on a sculpture . . . Taking the dust sheets from a bust of M. Zandomeneghi, who never comes to sit any more and is becoming more and more disagreeable, he said: 'That swine Zandomeneghi complained once to me: "Everyone does Degas' bidding; Bartholomé takes orders from him, but not me—I'll never give in to him!"'

The big, slightly crooked nose of Zandomeneghi was just beginning to appear, followed by the entire head—it's an absolute marvel.

'What a fine mug he has', commented M. Renoir.

Indeed there really is something quite superb in the movement of the mouth and the moustache. It has an extraordinary life of its own. Monsieur Degas seemed quite pleased with the likeness (which was understandable); he leant over the bust and observed it closely.

Monsieur Degas covered all his maquettes with wet cloths, then took off his cap and his white smock, put his shoes on, put on a jacket and a hooded cape, picked up his hat, and everyone went downstairs—M. Degas and his elderly friend arm in arm, while M. Degas told him about the death of his sister.

Then we went to Vollard's with M. Degas and M. Renoir to view the Cézanne exhibition. The still lifes appealed to me less than those I have seen so far; however there were some apples and a decorated pot in lovely colours. The nudes enveloped in blue are shielded by trees with light soft foliage. Monsieur Degas and M. Renoir drew lots for a magnificent still-life water-colour of pears and a small one depicting an assassination in the Midi which isn't in the least bit horrifying—the figures stand out in exactly the right tones, red, blue and violet in a landscape like that of Brittany and the Midi with rounded trees, areas of land drawn against a blue sea, and, in the background, some islands. Monsieur Renoir liked this very much too, so I bought it thinking it would be a sensible thing to do.

'Well look at this little art collector!' cried M. Degas, patting me affectionately under the chin. He gave me a kiss as we left and M. Renoir (who gives me the impression of being our protector) saw us on to the tram. He now has to go to his wife's part of the country to buy a house that he doesn't want to buy.

*Degas and his housekeeper, Zoë Clozier—a photograph taken by Degas himself in his apartment at
37 Rue Victor Massé, c. 1900*

Tuesday 3rd December

Paule is twenty-eight today. In fact I find this age very young, and younger still to be at the head of a household. Poor Paule—perhaps it's even harder for her than for us.

Pierre and Jean [Renoir] have both got chicken-pox and now I've got it; M. Renoir must have given it to me. I don't really feel ill but I'm not allowed to see anybody in case I give it to them.

I started copying a three-quarter profile head and shoulders of Maman in black, with a hat and a bouquet of violets on her bodice, by Oncle Edouard. Maman bought it at the Duret sale. It is hanging in my bedroom and I can see it from my

A 'pneumatique' from Renoir to Julie in January 1896 explaining that his sons have measles

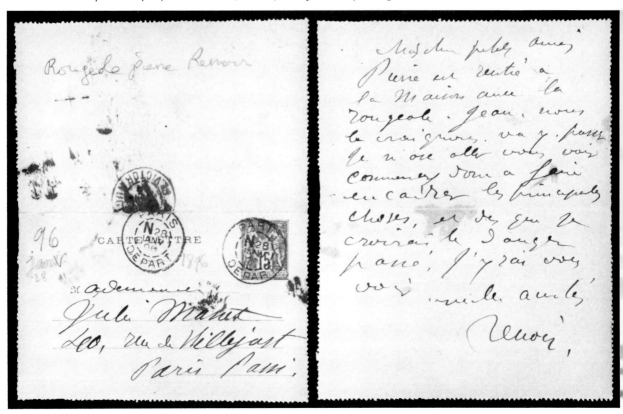

Renoir at Essoyes with his wife and son Claude, who was known as 'Coco', in 1909

bed; it's marvellous and magnificently executed, one would hardly believe that he did it in one or at the most two sittings. Maman told me she had sat for it during the day before one of the Thursday dinners that used to be held at Bonne-Maman's [Madame Marie-Cornélie Morisot]. That day Oncle Edouard told Maman that she ought to marry Papa and they talked about it for a very long time.

Em. Roussel

Additional notes written by Mme Ernest Rouart (Julie Manet) following a visit from Jean Renoir to Le Mesnil in August 1961

Jean Renoir and Dido came to spend the late afternoon and dine with us as they did on July 5th. Still as affectionate as ever, Jean spoke of the memoirs of his father which he is publishing (*Renoir* by Jean Renoir, Hachette).

We will always have plenty to say to each other on this subject; I told him about the months of August and September spent at Pont-Aven and Tréboul where we celebrated his first birthday with his parents in '95; all his father's kindness to my cousins and me, treating a crick in my neck with massage, giving up his painting umbrella so that we could get undressed on the beach, taking the trouble to come as far as Châteaulin ahead of us so that we would not have to spend a night alone at the hotel.

He forced himself to bathe so he could teach Pierre to swim and dive but became more and more uncomfortable in the water, so much so that Mme Renoir, who ran out of breath doing even a few strokes, acted as buoy and Pierre said to her,

'Maman, when you are seen from below, you're even fatter'. He was a delightful child, and used to trot off behind his father carrying a tiny basket saying, 'I'm going to do a very small sketch'.

Jean told me that his father was painting alongside Cézanne in March [1895] when Renoir heard the news of Maman's death. He closed his paintbox and took the next train back to Paris—I have never forgotten the way he arrived in my room in the Rue Weber and held me close to him; I can still see his white Lavallière cravat with its little red dots.

Paul Cézanne in Provence. Julie admired Cézanne's paintings of apples

OPPOSITE
Ernest Rouart *'Le Château du Mesnil'. Berthe Morisot hardly lived in the château acquired shortly before her husband's death, but it became Julie's home after her marriage and she brought up her three sons there*

1896

Edouard Manet *'Le Repos', depicting Berthe Morisot, painted in 1869*

Paul Durand-Ruel in the Rue Laffitte gallery, c. 1910

Monday 2nd March

It's the anniversary of that dreadful day when Maman suffered for the last time. It was harsh pain, both physical and mental. One year has slipped away already. It was cold then; the weather was in mourning, like our hearts. Today I alone have stayed in mourning, nature itself is cheerful. The yew trees in the cemetery were starkly outlined against the blue sky with wispy clouds, while the wreaths shone on the stone tombs. Beneath that huge green tree which sheltered Edouard Manet first of all, the azalea blended its immaculate whiteness with the delicate meadow-sweet and brightened up the granite. There was something reassuring about the tomb, which seemed to say that Maman was happy. . .

And later, going into the Durand-Ruel gallery [to prepare for the Berthe Morisot memorial exhibition], the paintings spread out on the floor gave me a feeling of brightness just as the white azalea had done.

Monsieur Monet was already there. He kissed me tenderly and I was very pleased indeed to see him again; it was very kind of him to come running over here like that, abandoning his work. Monsieur Degas was busy with the hanging; then Renoir arrived, not looking well. Among other tasks, M. Mallarmé had to go to the printers for the catalogue.

1896

Tuesday 3rd March

Another day spent at Durand-Ruel's. The paintings were all looking better and better. Monsieur Monet never stopped once. They asked for copies after Boucher, then the ones after Veronese, as well as others, as there is more room than one would have thought.

Wednesday 4th March to Friday 6th March

Went to Durand-Ruel's with Tante Edma and Blanche and took the bust with us. We found M. Degas all by himself putting up drawings in the room at the far end. He kept repeating constantly that he would have nothing to do with the public, those people who go around with wide eyes. looking at the paintings, or more precisely standing before them without seeing anything while declaring, 'Oh how beautiful! how very beautiful!'

Monsieur Monet chose the painting Maman left to him; he took one of me and Laërtes which I like very much and I'm very happy M. Monet has it now. He gave me a good-natured kiss saying, 'She's so sweet', and he's invited us to go to Giverny.

Madame Monet and Mlle Blanche arrived; Berthe [Butler, one of Alice Hoschedé-Monet's daughters] is still very ill. Lots of people have already attended since Monday. The critics Arsène Alexandre and Geffroy have been back frequently.

An installation view of the Impressionist still-life exhibition at the Durand-Ruel Gallery in April 1908, showing works by Renoir in what may be supposed to be similar conditions to those of the Berthe Morisot memorial exhibition in 1896. (Installation photographs were only made regularly after 1900 and this is the earliest such record available)

At the end of the day we were asking ourselves how on earth everything was going to be ready by the next day, and we arranged to meet in the morning; but a decision had to be made as to whether the screen should be put with the drawings and water-colours in the middle of the big gallery or in the one at the end.

Monsieur Degas was the only one who wanted the screen to remain in the big gallery where it cut the room into two and prevented one being able to view the large paintings such as the CERISIERS, the copy after Boucher, L'OIE, etc., in proper perspective, as well as other smaller ones whose tones look so harmonious next to each other when seen from a distance. Monsieur Degas wouldn't hear a word about the general effect: 'There's no such thing as the general effect', he said. 'Only imbeciles see a general effect. What on earth is it supposed to mean when one writes in a newspaper that the general impression of this year's Salon is much better than that of last year's?'

Towards 6 o'clock, night began to fall, only the paintings retaining a few rays of light which illuminated them; all those portraits of young girls seeming more and more alive and the screen even more of a barrier than ever. Monsieur Monet asked M. Degas if he wouldn't mind trying the infamous screen in the end gallery the next day, but M. Degas claimed that the drawings on it wouldn't be visible— 'Those drawings are superb, I think more of them than of all these paintings.'

'The screen in the gallery full of drawings would give it an intimate, quite charming atmosphere', said M. Mallarmé. 'It will confuse the public to see drawings in the middle of the paintings.'

'Do I care a jot about the public?' shouted M. Degas. 'They see nothing—it's for myself, for ourselves, that we are mounting this exhibition; you can't honestly mean that you want to teach the public to see?'

'Certainly I do', replied M. Monet, 'We want to try. If we put on this exhibition just for ourselves, it won't be worth going to the trouble of hanging all these paintings; we could quite simply look at them on the floor.'

During this discussion M. Renoir told us that what he wanted to do was put the couch in the middle of the room; in fact it would indeed be rather pleasant to be able to sit down while viewing but M. Degas wouldn't hear of it. 'I would stay on my feet for thirteen hours at a time if I had to', he shouted.

It was dark by then, and, as he spoke, M. Degas paced back and forth in his great hooded cape and top hat, his silhouette looking very comical; M. Monet, also on his feet, was beginning to shout; Mallarmé was trying to smooth things over; M. Renoir, exhausted, was stranded on a chair. The Durand-Ruel men were laughing, and declared, 'He'll never give in'. Mlle Blanche, Jeannie, and I were just listening.

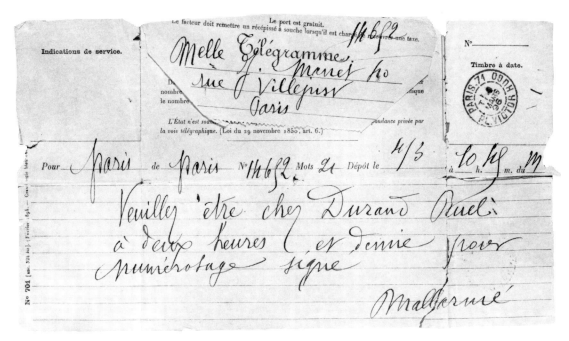

A telegram sent by Mallarmé to Julie Manet asking her to be present at the art dealer Durand-Ruel's to number her mother's work for the 1896 memorial exhibition

'You want me to remove this screen which I *adore*', M. Degas said, emphasizing the last word.

'*We* adore Mme Manet', retorted M. Monet. 'It's not a question of the screen, but one of Mme Manet's exhibition. Let's have it understood that we'll try the screen in the other room tomorrow.'

'If you can assure me that in your opinion the room is better without it.'

'Yes, that is my opinion!' stated Monet.

But that wasn't the end of it and the argument started up all over again. All of a sudden M. Degas shook hands with Jeannie and me and went towards the door. Monsieur Monet held him back and they shook hands; but M. Mallarmé hazarded the word 'couch' and, like a bolt of lightning, M. Degas rushed off into the narrow corridor. We heard the door slam and he'd gone. We left one another that evening a bit dumbfounded to say the least.

I arrived at Durand-Ruel's at 9 o'clock, but the only people there were the men sweeping the floors. I continued with my job of numbering the paintings and soon after M. Monet and M. Renoir arrived.

'You can bet Degas won't be coming', said M. Renoir. 'He'll be here later in the day up a ladder hammering away and will say, "Can't we put a cord across the door to prevent people from getting in?" I know him too well.'

1896

Sure enough, no M. Degas all morning. It was decided to put the screen in the end gallery and the water-colours and drawings were hung on it. At last everything was ready and beautifully arranged; the exhibition looked marvellous.

Julie then lists all the paintings in her mother's memorial exhibition, room by room, beginning in the small gallery on the Rue Laffitte side where all the early work was hung.

On the panel at the far end was SUR LA PELOUSE, a large pastel done at Maurecourt with Tante Edma, Blanche lying on the grass with her head leaning against her mother, and Jeanne farther away; the painting is in tones of green, from which the charming blonde and pink head of Blanche emerges. Above CHASSE AUX PAPILLONS, also done at Maurecourt with Tante Edma and her daughters. I was not familiar with these two pictures: the black patches of the dresses in the grass have an extraordinary value. On the right LE DÉJEUNER SUR L'HERBE, painted in Normandy at Beuzeval. Papa sat for that one—he's lying on the grass, the foreshortening is astonishingly well drawn; the figure of the woman in blue is full of graceful movement, her hand (even though this figure is tiny) is beautifully executed, taking an orange from a basket, the bread, carafe, glasses on a white napkin, all are equally well painted. I viewed this painting again with pleasure, the green of the grass is so soft that it envelops the figures well. Around it are [a number of other paintings including]: LE PETIT CERISIER, a more recent work. (A few of these have been put among the older ones and look well.) The branches of the cherry tree against the blue sky are the colours of precious stones.
——The still life ROSES DEVANT UNE GRAVURE, normally in Paule and Jeannie's bedroom, reminds me that I brought the roses back from Les Halles where the three of us went at four in the morning; that was about eight years ago.
——In the corner ETANG ET PIGEONNIER, a turret at Vassé jutting out over the pond, where the solitary reflections of the trees could be seen in the autumn of '92 during that week we spent there which seemed so long. Maman and I both sensed that same feeling of sadness in the huge château at the beginning of November; not to see Papa at Vassé among his family seemed ominous to me. 'When I was working on that', Maman said to me one day, showing me this delightful landscape, 'I couldn't stop myself from crying when I was alone in my room.' And in this reflection of trees in the grey water, one views the landscape through a veil of tears.
——VUE DE TOURS, the same year, very delicate pink tones.
——LE BASSIN DU PORT DE FÉCAMP, grey houses rising up in the distance above a foreground of wheat.
——LE CHANTIER: Papa and Maman both did the same study of this shipyard the year before their marriage; Maman gave what she had done to Papa. Then Portier asked for it; he didn't sell it and it was only two or three years ago that the little picture came back to the house and I saw it.
——ANGLETERRE, two charming English children in a meadow.
——L'AURORE, minute marine pastel, just a little boat on the pink sea. It's full of the

gaiety of sunrise over the immensity—the sea which from beautiful becomes pleasing or perhaps pretty; all pink, as is the sky and the sand on the beach on which rays of light from the heavenly body fall as it rises. Monsieur Monet thought this pastel was ravishing. I share his taste—besides quite a long time ago I asked if it could be mine, and Maman gave it to me as a present.

On the left: INTÉRIEUR, ÎLE DE WIGHT, PLAGE DE FÉCAMP, EN ANGLETERRE (the portrait of Papa in profile looking out of the window of a tiny cottage which overlooks the sea, with pots of flowers on the window-sill . . . this painting was done in '75 during the trip to England that Maman and Papa made after their wedding; it hangs in my bedroom and was in Maman's during the last few months of her life).
——MARINE D'ANGLETERRE, which M. Degas likes very much and which he washed with enormous care.

On the right-hand panel: In the middle, the big picture which usually hangs in the salon—Papa is sitting in profile on a bench in the garden at Bougival with me, when I was very small, playing at building a village on his knee; hollyhocks in brilliant colours behind us look like a fresco. It's painted on the back of a canvas.

Beneath it, CACHE-CACHE, Tante Edma and little Jeanne at Maurecourt around a tree laden with cherries; the village can be seen and in the grass is an open umbrella. Tante Edma has a green veil on her hat which has all the lightness of gauze.

To the right: ANÉMONES DANS UN CORNET DE VERRE—these flowers painted straight on to the canvas are simply delightful, the stems are marvellous.
——Next to it AU BAL, a woman with dark brown hair in a very low-cut gown, with a dull, dark violet flower on her bodice of white chiffon, wearing beautifully rendered white gloves and holding an equally well-painted and pretty fan. This is quite an old work, which I like enormously. I saw it for the first time in the '92 exhibition. It belongs to M. Donop de Monchy, who has lots of other equally ravishing things. It used to be hung in the dining-room of the Avenue d'Eylau apartment where Jeannie and I were born.
——Beneath it: PIGEONNIER DU MESNIL, done in '92, seen from the courtyard; the dovecote has all the qualities of old stone against a greenish blue tree which is both intense and soft at the same time.
——Next to that PORT DE NICE, a little light yellow boat is reflected in the blue water, with other bigger ones in all colours behind, and between the masts appear some pink houses. This was done during our first visit to Nice in '81. Maman painted in a boat out in the harbour and I watched from the quay, wishing I was with her and at the same time being very scared.

On the left-hand panel: In the centre, a portrait of Tante Edma (wearing a black dress) done in pastel before the birth of Blanche—it's a lovely thing.
——Underneath it the bas-relief in pewter of Marthe in a chemise with Jeanne-Marie at her feet.

——On a table in front of that, a marvellous bust of me at seven, in pink terracotta. Though of one so young, it's full of life.

——On the right: UN COIN DE PARIS VU DE L'ANCIEN TROCADÉRO with the Panthéon, Les Invalides, Ste Clothilde, Saint Sulpice magnificently drawn against the skyline and the Seine winding between the houses. In front of the Trocadéro lawn are two figures of women and a little girl. The whole thing is beautifully painted and in astonishing perspective.

On the wall with the door, to the right, is a copy of Veronese's LA DESCENTE DE LA CROIX, lovely, and accurate despite being done at the Louvre while the Veronese was hung very high up.

——Beneath it FEMME ET ENFANTS SUR LE GAZON, Tante Edma again with her baby daughters in the garden at Maurecourt; they're under lilac trees, with delightful flowers which envelop the figures in a marvellous green tone. It's one of the prettiest paintings, an old one like most of the ones here. Monsieur Degas found it at Stevens' house.

——On the left: TEMPS D'HIVER, a woman with a fur toque and coat against a snowy background.

——Beneath that VILLA AU BORD DE LA MER with Tante Edma and Jeanne on the terrace of a chalet at Fécamp against the green sea. In this painting one can see a certain similarity in the blacks and the sea to Oncle Edouard's technique. It's the only thing, despite what people say, in which I can see his influence; moreover, Maman only ever watched Oncle Edouard painting, she was never his pupil.

This little gallery which offers the viewer all the charming, intimate works of [Berthe Morisot's] youth, prepares one for going into the big gallery where, like a bouquet of the loveliest flowers the canvases seem to throw out rays of gentle sunshine. It seems as though one was going into another atmosphere. It's a paradise, with feminine delicacy combined with the power of the drawing. Ah, Maman, what talent! Your œuvre has never to me seemed as beautiful as it did today; it's the reflection of a pure soul! One must be inspired by God to produce all this, and certainly the greatest artists are always the most virtuous of men; no talent without goodness or goodness so great it replaces all else. Miss Vos used to say to me: 'All of us have something of the Divine in us, God gives to each one a little of himself; some acquire more of this divinity through goodness, duty, work, talent; and the beautiful and superb things man makes are divine. God gives us this consolation.' What a difference it makes for me to mourn Maman surrounded by all these things which she created and which embody herself. Going into these rooms where her glory shines forth, I feel she is happy in heaven. Oh Maman, inspire me!

This is how the big gallery is arranged: The panel on the right (going in via the Rue Laffitte):

Berthe Morisot *Edma Pontillon, the artist's sister*

——In the middle a copy after Boucher, two Graces in the clouds, completely enveloped in blue and pink.

——VÉNUS VA DEMANDER LES ARMES À VULCAIN, from the big painting in the Louvre, which was done after we moved into the Rue de Villejust in about '83 or '84 to be put in the white salon above the huge Louis XIV mirror. But some years later this copy was replaced by a big landscape by Monet done in the Midi, which is now above the door in our salon as a pendant to the Boucher.

——On the right, the version of LE CERISIER which was worked on the most, begun at Mézy, with Jeannie below holding the basket and me on the ladder picking cherries. It was finished in the Rue Weber apartment with a very nice model, and Jeannie stayed as she was. The sky is that of a hot day, with the arms of the upper figure in silhouette against it, and the branches of the cherry tree marvellously drawn. The pink dress reflects the green tones of the tree, and the sweetness of the atmosphere envelops the brilliant patches of light here and there on the dress. The lower figure in a lovely straw hat is also enveloped in green.

——LE CERISIER on the left was worked on in the Rue Weber between the beginning and finishing of the other one. The sky is bluer, the greens above more brilliant, the upper figure is in a white dress with pink flowers and is less in shadow and has the arms raised higher; the lower figure is also wearing a lighter coloured dress. Lots of people don't know which of the two pictures they prefer; they hesitate, and are of divided opinion. Monsieur Degas likes no. 3 and M. Renoir likes that better as a whole, but prefers parts of the other. Monsieur Monet admires both of them. Monsieur Mallarmé prefers no. 2 and so do I; perhaps that's because Maman considered it by far the better and had spent more time on it. [There were two versions of LE CERISIER in oil and one in watercolour in the exhibition, as well as three preparatory works.]

Last January, Camentron took this painting away to sell it. Maman was only asking 1,500 francs but when he had gone she wished she hadn't given it to him and wrote to Camentron asking him to return it. The latter claimed to have promised it already, was very unpleasant, and demanded a commission of 150 francs, which Maman gave him in order to get it back. The purchaser was my cousin Gabriel Thomas, but he hadn't made a pledge, so everything sorted itself out. Maman promised to paint something decorative especially for him.

When the LE CERISIER was returned to the little studio in the Rue Weber, Mama said: 'I did the right thing not to sell it. I worked on it for so long at Mézy, during your father's last year; I'll keep it and after my death you will be pleased to have it.' In a month she was dead and it made me feel better to look at this delicious work which now hangs in our salon opposite L'OIE, and every day I contemplate it and repeat to myself that phrase. Ah! when Maman said that to me how could I think that death was so near her, only a month more to be with her. How we need God's grace to bear it!

——Then PAYSANNE NIÇOISE, a sort of brown-haired savage with huge black eyes, a small blue bodice, carrying a rose, and in the background the mountains which border the Var; quite admirable those dark eyes against the skin; what lustre! When we got back from Nice, Maman showed it to M. Gigoux, who thought it was a portrait of me: 'There she is all right, that dear little thing', said he, 'but she is so shabbily dressed.'

——Also a copy after Boucher (NYMPHES D'APOLLON VISITANT LATONE), a painting which is in the museum at Tours; Maman reproduced the grace and suppleness of the nymphs exactly, as well as the dark, matt woods behind them. It makes me think of the first line of *L'Après-midi d'un Faune* by M. Mallarmé—'Ces nymphes, je les veux perpétuer si clair, leur incarnat léger . . . etc.'

——LES PÂTÉS DE SABLES, Bibi [Julie] in a pink dress with a little brown bonnet, making sand pies at Bougival—which for me was ultimate happiness. 'If your Maman was lost', Maman asked me, 'what would you do?' 'I'd play in the sand', I replied innocently.

——SOMNOLENCE, with a model who I used to call 'the Monster' but who isn't at all monstrous in this canvas, wearing a pink dress against a red background of Japanese door-curtains.

——My portrait, in a pale rose dress against a background of door-hangings with dark beads. I have a side parting and an orange bow, a very round Egyptian-looking face, red lips, a string of pearls around my neck, hands so daintily small, a turquoise ring. I am holding on my lap an antique book (a copy of Racine) and I am reciting 'Come hither, Nero, and take your place, etc. . . .' This portrait is extremely unusual, there is something both stiff and supple about it at the same time.

On the left-hand side (entering by Rue Laffitte): In the centre LA VÉRANDA, which has belonged to M. Chausson since the '92 exhibition. It used to be hung when we lived in the Rue Princesse [at Bougival] above the piano. It's big, and was sold for 300 francs. I'm in the glazed dining-room, with my blonde hair, playing at a table where there are some beautifully painted flowers in a carafe. The background of very blue trees, between which is the roof of a house, is delicious.
——Below this is the portrait of Maman by herself, an admirable sketch, which is not embellished in any way; but one can see from it what a great artist she was, full face with her grey hair, some black around the neck and rather yellowish bodice bordered with flowers, of which one is 'like a medal' as M. Mallarmé put it—which gives her a chivalrous air, or so M. de Régnier thought. This portrait was done about ten years ago. Maman didn't finish it. No one ever saw it; she rolled it up and left it in a wardrobe or store-room—its appearance at the exhibition is a cause for wonderment.

——At the side: JEUNE FILLE AU LÉVRIER, showing me in the Rue Weber drawing-room, in front of a Japanese print, and seated on the beige velvet sofa in a black silk frock, leaning slightly towards Laërtes who is in front of me showing his rounded back. This is the marvellous picture M. Monet chose [now in the Musée Marmottan, Paris].

——LE CORSAGE ROUGE is on the stand in the corner—Isabelle, her fresh face standing out from a huge round straw hat. She's sitting in the middle of a flower-bed of pansies and behind her is a bird-cage. How well I can see Maman working at this beautiful garden. Papa did a water-colour of it too; and this painting was exhibited at the Impressionist exhibition at Petit's gallery, hanging next to M. Renoir's beautiful bathers and as pendant to the portrait of Paule. These two with their reds and pinks went very well together.

——Beneath it LA PETITE MARCELLE—these were the last brushstrokes Maman ever made. Here is her last work, this little girl in a light-coloured frock against a back-drop of pink Japanese door-hangings, standing by an Empire armchair; this little creature whose face with its huge, sad, dark eyes is surrounded with hair. Maman loved children, youth; and for the last time, she painted a little girl. But this one isn't laughing like those of yesteryear; it isn't Nini [Jeanne Gobillard], or Bibi with her happy personality; no, this one is sad, profoundly sad, she is in the presence of death. Oh, what a dear and yet sad keepsake for me! I didn't see Maman working on it for the last time—I was ill and in bed the day she took up her palette for the last time. It was two weeks before leaving us:

Oh triste petite Marcelle,	(Oh sad little Marcelle
Tes yeux noirs regardent la mort	your black eyes contemplate death
Et tu restes la gloire de celle	and you remain the glory of one
Qui, entourée de clarté, dort	who, surrounded by light, sleeps
Laissant comme exemple une si belle	leaving as an example so lovely
Œuvre; belle jusqu'à sa mort!	an œuvre, beautiful unto death)

——LA FLEUR AUX CHEVEUX (M. Mallarmé gave it this pretentious title, which I don't like much; the same as *La Fable*). Once again Jeanne-Marie dressing Marthe's hair; with Marthe leaning her head back a little, full face, fresh complexioned, her neck and chest emerging from a light froth of pink chiffon. Jeanne-Marie, with blonde hair and lowered eyes, dressed in a Turkish tunic in white chiffon embroidered in gold, is putting white flowers into her dark hair; a few red anemones tumble over the white dress and a ravishing blue hydrangea is in a Japanese porcelain vase. What a beautiful light, colourful canvas! I remember working alongside Maman in the studio in the Rue Weber when she did it. [This picture is now known as L'HORTENSIA.]

——LE VIOLIN: I'm in a black dress with a white belt, facing the artist. The violin is admirably foreshortened; the background is the white, slightly greenish salon in the Rue Weber; on the wall are hanging the portrait of Papa by M. Degas and the portrait of Maman by Oncle Edouard.

——The portrait of Paule, in a pink ball-gown against a grey background, sitting on a grey sofa—her almost blonde hair caught up with a huge Japanese comb. The face is very pretty, a good likeness, quite pale, and lit in a rather unusual way with a green light; the eyes are as charming as Paule's are in real life. This portrait was exchanged for some Japanese prints a few years ago and now Hayashi, the Japanese collector, has agreed to give it back in return for DERRIÈRE LA JALOUSIE and the drawing of MARTHE EN CHEMISE.

The panel on the left of the left-hand panel: In the middle:
——FILLETTE AU PANIER, marvellous big canvas with Cocotte, in a white chiffon hat bordered with lace which falls slightly over her eyes, in a very pale pink dress sitting on a straw chair holding a basket. She is in the green dining-room, a delightful green, and on the dresser there are some apples and a delft sugar basin. This magnificent work belongs to my cousin Gabriel. Maman was working on it in '92 when Papa was ill and stayed in his room; when Cocotte arrived, Maman, who was keeping Papa company, came downstairs to work, with a troubled spirit.
——Beneath that the portrait of Lucie Léon, which was done in the summer of the same year, in the same house, in the Rue Princesse—but Papa was no longer there; he had left us and everything was dilapidated, the big drawing-room was empty. It was hot and Lucie would have preferred to play croquet rather than to pose at the piano; she was an unbearable model but, as Maman overcame every difficulty, she created a marvellous portrait—all blue like the 'Blue Boy' by Gainsborough. Lucie's head is framed by her thick brown hair, with big, rather sad blue eyes, red mouth and small nose. She is wearing a light blue dress with short puffed sleeves; her arms, which are quite chubby and round, circled with a gold bracelet, are admirably painted. Leaning forward a little, she is playing a mahogany piano upon which a lace handkerchief has been placed and, on the top, three beautiful roses tied with a blue ribbon. All this against a dark blue background strewn with peacock feathers. This portrait of Lucie reminds me of the little girl in blue at the piano by David which is in the museum in Le Mans and which was in the big exhibition in '89. What a lovely portrait! Lucie is jolly lucky to have this magnificent work of art after doing nothing to deserve it.

In the long room at the end are all the drawings and especially the sketches, mixed in with pastels of the gardens at Le Mézy and at Cimiez (Niçoises under the orange trees, charming heads of children). They go very well next to the red chalk drawings and the charcoal sketches. The works in coloured pencil and watercolour are almost all on the screen, which takes up half the gallery and looks very successful.

It is impossible for me to write about every single thing: I would never get it finished. What clarity in her drawing! What lovely impressions of landscapes these things in coloured pencil are, the use of which Maman alone had made her art; and what delightful watercolours, which are so special to her! Everyone is astonished on coming into this room, exclaiming: 'I would never have believed she did so much work.' They say that Maman never showed all these drawings, that she hid part of her work. Today it comes as a revelation.

On arrival in the little gallery one is struck by the scholarship in these works from her youth and the precision of the drawing; in the big gallery, by the clarity and the extraordinary light of the painting which illuminate the room, by the supple, delightful figures, the marvellous tones of the flowers—this œuvre is so feminine and so consistent. In the room at the far end it is the drawing which fills you with wonder, and the workmanship; a soul so completely that of an artist shows itself as much in the slightest sketch as in the most elaborate canvas.

A concert programme dated 11 June 1896, in which Julie and her cousins are listed as performers

Undated

Monsieur Mallarmé dined with us and charmed us with his conversation.

'Mistral told me', he said, 'that he had only been shooting once in his life. Being armed with a rifle and pursuing a hare, he aimed at it; but it turned round and made the sign of the cross. Mistral dropped his rifle and never touched a firearm again.'

Saturday 3rd October

We went to do some shopping and passed along the Champs Elysées, which is being decorated rather nicely for the Tzar's visit. At the Rond-Point all the trees have artificial white, pink and red flowers, which shine in the sun and are almost the same as real flowers; a row of white globes borders the avenue on each side.

Street decorations for the state visit of Tzar Nicholas II to Paris in October 1896

In the evening we read with Jeannie some letters from Bon-Papa [grandfather Morisot] to Tante Yves—there are lots of really lovely ones and quite a few lectures. In one of them the following rather amusing family portrait: 'Berthe seems always to be astonished; I don't know if it's by others or by herself. Edma makes fun of her mother all week long and usually spends Sundays fighting and then making it up with her brother. This charming child continues to blow his own trumpet and dictate to us. As for me, I try to ignore it all, or else I grumble. Our petty problems seem to have a negative effect on M. Guichard. . .'

I enjoy re-reading family letters, but the handwriting is difficult to understand. In one of them Bon-Papa speaks of an evening when he had a great deal of trouble getting Maman to come in from the garden. She was fourteen and wanted to spend the night out of doors and ended up in tears; she often spoke to me of that evening. Bon-Papa found her very secretive and asked Tante Yves to tell him if she knew any of Maman's little secrets.

Monday 5th October

Went shopping in Paris this morning. The streets were decorated with flags and garlands, and red and yellow celluloid balloons were strung across the boulevards.

After lunch, went to M. Bouts [their banker] with Paule; as we left, Paule dropped the 1,000 francs she had just withdrawn; so there we were on all fours on the pavement gathering up the pieces of gold which surrounded us. I was laughing so much that I dropped them as fast as I could pick them up. The passers-by looked at us in amazement—what a ridiculous situation! M. Bouts said we could go and see the fireworks tomorrow evening from a house in the Avenue Malakoff which he manages, and M. Mallarmé was kind enough to ask for places for us on Dr Evans' balcony to see the arrival of the Tsar tomorrow morning.

Tuesday 6th October

This was the opportunity to put on my grey fur cloak and my big feathered velvet hat. We were on the balcony early to see if the crowd had already gathered on the Avenue du Bois and if it was time to leave. Clouds gave way to the sun; we admired our three large flags linked together by a cordon of ten small scarlet banners [oriflammes], the whole flapping about, the lanterns swaying in the wind.

We made our way to Dr Evans' big house on the corner of the Avenue du Bois and Rue de la Pompe, where we were shown into a room which gave on to the drawing-room; there we found Mme Marguerite, her sons, and her nieces. The balcony wasn't too crowded; one could see the avenue very well; Dr Evans came in

More street decorations for the state visit of Tzar Nicholas II

from time to time; he really organizes things very well. We thus spent about an hour, chatting.

The crowd became dense along the avenue but was kept in order, with soldiers lining the street. In the side lanes endless carriages barred the way. They had evidently decided that the avenue was splendid enough on its own, so there were just a few little banners in different colours criss-crossed among the still-green trees. We heard some oohs and ahs, and wondered what it was. A panic-stricken dog was tearing along the middle of the avenue, finding no escape route on either side, and never has a poor creature been so heartily applauded. Later on another went by, but this one looked miserable with its tail between its legs, passing along slowly, which still did not prevent it receiving an ovation. From time to time horses with soldiers on them galloped past in the direction of the Bois towards Ranelagh station where the Tsar was arriving.

At last an ordinary carriage went by with a gentleman twiddling his moustache; then, a short while later, another also twiddling his moustache. This was it! 'Ah, ah, ooh!' the crowd went when the procession appeared, with many army corps at the front, riflemen, hussars all in blue and mounted on lovely white horses; then Algerian troopers in their turbans, their clothing in the most delicious tones of almond green, red, yellow, with greatcoats which flapped in the wind, riding ravishing Arab steeds, whose hindquarters were covered in embroidered fabrics of the most magnificent colours and which trailed on the ground. One would have thought one was looking at a Delacroix when one of these horses reared a little, so proud of its royal mantle. What a treat for the eye! It was beautiful to observe this luminous battalion through the branches of the trees; it seemed to have taken on the colours of the most brilliant flowers or the most beautiful jewels.

Preceded by Montjaret, the Imperial carriage appeared. On the right the Tsarina all in white, on the left the Tsar, and in front on the folding seat poor old Félix Faure, as red as a beetroot, seemingly very embarrassed to be where a child is usually seated—and his knees came right up to his chin. Other carriages followed: one was filled with ladies in white and mauve chiffon, the ladies-in-waiting of the Empress. Cavalry squadrons brought up the rear of the procession.

As soon as the Tsar was some distance away, the crowd, which had been very well behaved, swarmed everywhere, spread out and rushed about. How well my Oncle Edouard painted crowds; it's quite extraordinary, that dominant violet tone which he managed to imbue with movement.

After dinner we went to 11 Avenue Malakoff, where a kindly concierge gave us a candle and told us to go up to the fifth floor. After waiting for a time, different coloured rockets were set off round the Eiffel Tower, lighting up the whole sky and going up more than 300 metres high. They all exploded at the same time and seemed to be vying with one another for the honour of going higher than the flag on top of the tower. Sometimes showers of pure gold sparks whirled around, seeming to fight with each other; then some huge, luminous blue stars juggled above the roof-tops and let themselves be carried away on the breeze while diamonds fell from the sky. The Eiffel Tower was aflame with red. Then suddenly a rain of fire fell from the first platform, then the second, and finally the third. It was surrounded by pure gold, a golden tower standing out against the sky. The wind carried this shower away and a huge cloud of pink smoke floated towards Paris. Out of this marvellous fire appeared an image of Saint George on the second platform of the tower. Everything went out. Then a bouquet followed by other rockets crowned this marvellous firework display.

The banks of the Seine decorated in celebration of Tsar Nicholas II's visit

OVERLEAF

The magnificent firework display given on the occasion of the Tsar's state visit to Paris in October 1896. Julie describes the scene in great detail in her diary

1896

Thursday 8th October

We tried once again to see the other bank of the river and we succeeded this time. A crowd was at the entrance to the Solférino bridge. They were waiting for the Tsar; so we waited too, for a very long time. We rented chairs, on which we climbed, and from there were able to see the sovereigns fairly well. The Emperor was blond and looked very young; the Empress looked rather stiff and had a big nose.

We went along the *quais* in front of the proposed Pont Alexandre III (by the way, the ceremony last evening must have looked beautiful). At 2 o'clock the Tsar went by in a carriage pulled by six white horses along the Avenue du Bois and we saw him from our balcony. The crowd seemed to be very enthusiastic; we heard lots of cheering. After the Emperor had passed by, all the people who had made their final adieux to him poured into the Rue de Villejust, which had never before teemed with so many people. We had a visit from my cousin Gabriel [Thomas], who told us that the firework display had gone wrong—that's perhaps why it was so pretty.

Sunday 18th October

Lunched at Montmartre at the Renoirs, who are always very pleasant. Jean has taken on the look of a little girl. Monsieur Renoir has rented a superb studio in Rue de la Rochefoucauld.

Thursday 31st December

A charming day to end the year 1896, during which thank God we haven't had any further misfortunes. I ask only that it is the same in '97.

Monsieur Renoir came to see us at the same time as M. Mallarmé, who brought each of us a box of bonbons with a charming quatrain. He has done so for me for the last nine years. This one is very pretty, particularly sweet and 'Mallarmé'. We kissed him, and took the opportunity to kiss M. Renoir too.

It was lovely to see the spirited painter and the charming poet chatting together as they have so often done at our house on those Thursday evenings in the high-ceilinged pink salon, where the hosts, in their own surroundings, were among those they loved, among precious friends.

It made me think of M. Renoir's comment, which touched Maman deeply when it was repeated to her. The poet and the painter were on their way home after dinner and part of the evening spent with Maman, and were talking about her charming way with guests. 'It must be said that any other woman with everything she has would find a way of being quite unbearable', said M. Renoir.

Renoir, his wife, and baby Claude in 1901

1897

Julie Manet *Jeanne Baudot painting in the studio at 40 Rue de Villejust*

Monday 1st February

Paule took me into Paris today by carriage. We went to see M. Renoir at his studio. He is working on some delightful guitar studies: a woman in a white chiffon dress which is held in position with pink bows leaning gracefully over the big yellow guitar, with her feet on a yellow cushion; another canvas is of a man in a Spanish costume who seems to be playing lively tunes on his instrument. The whole effect is colourful, mellow, delicious. Monsieur Renoir was charming, affectionate, and likeable as a woman never would be.

We stopped at Mlle Baudot's studio. She is working with a rather nice model and showed us several things, among which were some seascapes with well-painted boats, freely done, very well-drawn—it's quite astonishing for someone of her age to do it.

Wednesday 10th February

I went to a concert with Paule and we then went to see M. Degas, who seemed to be in low spirits because of his health—he has something wrong with his lungs and must be very careful.

There are some lovely things in his studio. He spoke of M. Mallarmé's delightful conversation; then said that these days everyone seems to be a poet. If he goes into a salon where there are some young people and asks one of them what he does, 'poet' is the reply, and another will answer 'poet' too, all poets. 'Remember', he said to us, that marvellous phrase of L.P. Fargues': "Once upon a time there was a young man, so handsome, so very handsome, that women expressly wanted him to write"?'

Paule ventured to say that M. Mallarmé disdained women.

'But women always think they're disdained when, on the contrary, they're our only concern; they're our chief problem, women', he replied.

Wednesday 28th July

Receiving no reply from the de Vaissières to whom I had written to say that we were on our way to see them, we decided to go for a short trip in Touraine. Just before leaving this morning, I received a letter from Tante de V. saying that she is expecting us on Tuesday, so we have a week to travel round in the heat.

We visited Orléans and went for a walk beside the Loire, which is very depressing at Orléans; then left the town with relief, arriving at Blois about six in the evening.

Paule Gobillard, Julie's cousin, in her twenties

At Blois we went to the Couvent de la Providence where the little Chassaing girl is. Paule asked the Mother Superior if she would accept us as paying guests, and she replied that she would as we had come on the recommendation of Mlle Manet. 'But this *is* Mlle Manet'—'Oh, how can it be? So young, Mademoiselle, to be engaged in charitable works—I thought Mlle Manet was an elderly person.' I suppose that, because of the letters I wrote to the convent, they must have thought I was an old girl of 70.

We decided that we wouldn't go to the convent until the next day and spent the night at the hotel instead, where there were some rather charming young men for us.

From the Loire Valley, Julie and her cousins travel to her aunt at Vassé, where she spends some time.

Thursday 12th August

Still at Vassé. Our stay here is wonderful, being entertained so well by these people who leave you free yet are simply charming. That is until today, when things went

Julie Manet *Springtime landscape*

less well, the reason being a book. It's jolly unlucky as we read only rarely, especially Paule who doesn't enjoy it much.

This year the idea occurred to me to bring a stack of books. Among them was *À Rebours* by Huysmans [*Against Nature*, which caused a sensation when it was published in 1884] for Paule to look at before I read it, as I had been attracted by the title. My cousin Marie was also fascinated by the title, and, seeing it in our case, took it; then thought nothing more of it until this morning when my aunt returned the book while we were walking in the park, saying it was horrible, that she didn't want Georges to see it, etc.

Paule naturally enough was quite annoyed for, although I explained that it was my book, Paule, being the eldest, will have to take the blame. What rotten luck!

September – undated

ESSOYES [AT THE RENOIRS']
I read a few pages of Marie Bashkirtseff's diary this morning, as I didn't have time to finish it on the journey. It's really very interesting to read the diary of an intelligent young woman with an open mind; she is curious, not at all disagreeable as I had believed from what I had heard others say of her. Underneath it all she isn't so vainglorious, though she does tend to force herself into a certain character and without a doubt she has plenty of imagination. If she says time and again that her own painting is good, it's to persuade herself that it is for she is nonetheless

aware that she paints badly. She evidently had a natural aptitude for many things, perhaps too many, for if she had been taught well she would probably have done something good.

But among bad painters, from a family who understood nothing about art, what could she do? What a sad life, without misfortunes, but sad because she had the sort of personality which created problems for herself; she was far too advanced— at twelve she was already speaking like an eighteen year old.

What infuriates me about her is that, living at a time when Manet and all the Impressionists were alive, she had nothing to say about any of that. This need to succeed young, this ambition, must have been the product of knowing that her life was to be a short one. What an interesting person; funny, too. Her dialogues with the famous A. at Rome when she was fifteen are very pretty and amusing.

Thursday 16th September

Monsieur Renoir came to fetch us before dinner. We showed him what we had been doing. He told me that my dahlias were good—it gives me great pleasure if he really thinks so; then he said that my 'Dina holding the basket' was badly drawn, that I should start again. I had indeed noticed that she was too short, but was simply niggling away at the same canvas. I'm glad M. Renoir has told me to start it again—it helps to have some advice. Monsieur Renoir told me that it was ridiculous not to be able to distinguish what was good from what was bad. In saying my dahlias were quite splendid, he told me I should leave them turned to the wall for a week and then I would be able to judge them myself. It seems to me that I need more and more time to find out how I'm doing, and to realize that, usually, it's badly. What I would really like would be for M. Renoir to give me advice often.

Until now I was very ambitious—I wanted to have real talent. Now I want only to be more than the young girl who paints fans and blinds, and perhaps in due course I won't even have that ambition. The greatest glory isn't a virtue; we should do what we can and do it well and we will be satisfied. Pleasing God is really the only true happiness.

Friday 17th September

Monsieur Renoir unbandaged his arm this evening. I was frightened at the sight of all those hairs—how ugly men are! An animal has a fur coat, but men have hairs which leave the skin visible, it's horrible! One certainly needs plenty of courage to marry them.

Sunday 19th September

Spent part of the day writing an interminable letter in English to Miss Vos [an English acquaintance of the Manet family].

Monday 20th September

M. Renoir told us that after the war, as a soldier, he spent two months in a château where he was treated like a prince, giving painting lessons to the young lady of the family and riding about on horseback all day. They didn't want to let him leave, fearing he would be killed during the Commune.

Wednesday 22nd September

'In life it's the same as in art', says M. Renoir, 'everything is a matter of comparison.' He is putting up with his broken arm very well, declaring that he'd rather have that than something else.

Tuesday 28th September

Monsieur Renoir attacked all the latest mechanical contraptions, saying that we are living in an age of decadence where people think of nothing but travelling at dozens of kilometres an hour; that it serves no useful purpose; that the automobile is an idiotic thing; that there is no need to go so fast; that the whole thing will mean change; that for work and business there must be a sort of compromise. The government is more autocratic than ever with mechanization, which does everything. The labourer is no longer capable of thought, of bettering himself; those without the means will always stay at the same level. Whatever is the point of going so fast? The gentleman who has a factory making 100,000 pairs of socks per day can't always find an outlet for them, and after a time the factory cannot keep going, so we have to sell socks to the savages, and persuade them that they have to wear socks in order to keep some gentleman's factory going. We want to conquer in order to sell our products. Slavery has been abolished but this is worse than slavery; the labourer who knows he cannot improve his lot knows that he will always remain the same and probably be more unhappy than the slave.

Isn't M. Renoir right? What a sound mind, always saying such sensible things. This mechanization which is invading the entire world is overwhelming. I watch the arrival of the automobile with horror. Bicycles, although I think there are far too many of them, I find less awful; however I can't say anything further against them as I am learning to ride one. Monsieur Renoir, who broke his arm dismounting, must hate them.

1897

Monday 11th October

It's pleasant to go for a walk with a talented, witty man who talks to you as though he doesn't find you too stupid (besides, intelligent men are indulgent with young people). I went for a lovely walk alone with M. Renoir, from Essoyes to Verpillière, and back. It's a pretty route to take in this weather. Today it was an autumnal grey, with blues in the background and with lilac and grey trees, mellow, like something from Corot or Renoir.

Monsieur Renoir was filled with admiration. 'Ah! I don't know if you're like me', he said, 'each time I go for a walk without my paintbox, I find a heap of places to paint, when I only have to take it in order not to find anywhere.'

Coming back by the main road, we met a woman with a pannier on her back. 'How well Corot painted those figures!' cried M. Renoir. 'How well he understood the little white bonnet! How well the people from the last century portrayed the landscape—it's not done like that any more. Watteau painted his backgrounds so well—only blue in the atmosphere today, it's like velvet.'

On the subject of the walk to Clairvaux, M. Renoir told me: 'If one was never ill, one wouldn't enjoy health; if it didn't rain, one wouldn't enjoy fine weather. One has to see things that are less attractive from time to time; the pleasure in life is the element of surprise. When I was young, I used to go to Fontainebleau with Sisley with just my paintbox and a shirt. We would walk until we found a village, and sometimes only come back a week later when we had run out of money.'

Monsieur Renoir also told me that it was at Fontainebleau that he first met Pissarro, who at that time was quite swarthy, and that he mistook him for an accordion player.

We also talked about the Natansons. Monsieur Renoir said it was very dangerous to support anarchists such as Fénéon, who busy themselves with literature while awaiting an opportunity to throw themselves into politics and who will end up by doing something terrible. He must be right. Writers support too many bad causes, whereas painters are of sounder mind. Pissarro, however, is an anarchist.

Thursday 14th October

Before leaving, M. Renoir told me that my new 'Dina' is well proportioned but, curiously, I found this less encouraging than when he told me it was out of proportion.

At the moment I can't think of anything except painting. I have heaps of other things to do, yet I'm starting a picture of three lovely fish from the Ource. I'm completely taken with painting, and am working hard at it these days. I am upset to think that in Paris I won't have the benefit of M. Renoir's advice as I do here. I think that, generally speaking, I lack direction; but I can't imagine that M. Renoir would ever be interested in me.

Saturday 16th October

Unexpectedly autumn has appeared with its golden trees; and how lovely the sunset was after the rain had stopped. It was absolutely a Degas landscape—with his great lines for the hillsides, his tones, the rapport between the green meadows and the yellow trees. Madame Renoir and Jean had lunch with us; Jean is sweet with his red hair against the russet trees.

Sunday 17th October

Magnificent weather. Jeannie decided to go out in the carriage; we installed ourselves as well as we could, and went as far as Grancey. The wild cherry trees were scarlet against the blue sky and made pretty splashes against the yellow trees. Going into Burgundy on the Côte d'Or it seemed as though one had entered a golden country; at Grancey the river was spangled with gold and with the ravishing blue of the sky. It is all very beautiful. I would love to be able to record these tones but will be leaving on Tuesday; no more time to do anything.

Last dinner at Essoyes with Mme Renoir.

Friday 22nd October

For some time now I haven't been feeling quite as usual. I seem to be asking myself less often 'What shall I do?' Faivre's teasing did me a lot of good—it brightened me up. I think one needs men in life, they give one a wider outlook. I do think it's better to marry than to remain a spinster—anyway, didn't God create the world to grow from generation to generation?

TOP LEFT
Julie Manet *Self-portrait, probably copied from one of Berthe's Morisot's numerous studies of this subject*

TOP RIGHT
Julie Manet *Jeannie Gobillard at the piano*

BOTTOM
Julie Manet *Jeannie Gobillard at Le Mesnil*

Jeannie always says it's a duty to marry and have children; but, as for this duty, does it go as far as marrying someone you don't like just to populate France? If this is the case, it's a very harsh requirement. It has always struck me that introductions and marriages by arrangement must be odious, but to be loved and to love must be wonderful. I don't think I will ever taste this happiness, it would be too much for me. I don't expect any great joy in my life, yet I'm hoping there might be a little bit all the same. . .

Thursday 28th October

Reading the diary of Marie Bashkirtseff, it always astonishes me to think that she lived until recently. She recounted the death of Gambetta which I remember so well. I was four then and went to the Palais Bourbon on the 4th January when his body was lying in state. I can remember the masses of draperies and wreaths—it made a great impression on me.

The second volume of Marie Bashkirtseff's diary is really sad; she felt keenly that her end was nigh. But there are some very interesting things in it and only the stories about the ateliers and her admiration for bad painters annoy me. I remember that Papa and Maman were reading this diary at Mézy; they talked about it a good deal and had numerous discussions on the subject. Papa, far from thinking like M. Degas that Marie Bashkirtseff was a woman who ought to be flogged in public, admired her. Maman teased him: 'I can just see you with a woman like that—you would find her unbearable.' And indeed what a difference between her and Maman, full of talent and so straightforward, charming and yet not seeming to be aware of the fact. She must have found Marie Bashkirtseff extraordinary, but I do not think she should be judged by what she said. She really couldn't have been as conceited as she seems.

After spending the summer in M. Renoir's company, I am struck with the thought that one ought to know how to do a little of everything, and be skilful at it—M. Renoir repeats this constantly and one gets it into one's head eventually. He has a great deal of influence over the young people who admire him, and says such philosophical things, so charmingly, that one automatically believes them. If only all men of his age could have as good an influence over young people. . .

Monsieur Mallarmé doesn't give enough advice. He could give ethical advice in the most delightful manner, and he has such a worthy lifestyle (M. Renoir greatly admires his character) that he ought to guide young people; instead of which he is over-indulgent with them. It has been said that youth profits in no way from the advice of the elderly, but I think this is incorrect. Even if one appears not to be benefiting, at least one thinks about it a good deal—men of ability should lead the young.

Tuesday 16th November

Spent the whole day at the Louvre. Jeanne [Jeanne Baudot, artist and lifelong friend of Julie's] was doing a very nice loose sketch of a Veronese. We saw lots of people there, including Carolus Duran with his large stomach sticking out and looking very commonplace. (When he went past, the guards asked us if we knew this 'great painter'.)

Monsieur Mallarmé, who arrived shortly afterwards with Whistler, said: 'He's decided to honour the Louvre with a visit during his own lifetime.' Whistler either heard nothing, or pretended not to understand, but what he did notice were the steel buttons on the sleeves of my dress.

We also saw Zandomeneghi go by with his huge Italian nose, which he glued to the Primitives.

When M. Renoir arrived I told him I had seen his friend, Z. He shouted: 'Quick, warn the guards that he's about to steal a painting so he can take it back to Venice!' Then, putting on his Italian accent, he imitated him proclaiming that the paintings in the Louvre by Italian masters were among people who understood nothing at all about them.

Monsieur Renoir said not a word to Jeanne about her copy. She had worked so hard on it, thinking she would probably see him. For some reason he gave me far more attention, saying mine was good and that Veronese was a good choice to copy, and that, if I didn't do well, he'd write to M. Caliari. Then he asked me if it bothered me to work in the Louvre.

Indeed, one would have thought I was his pupil rather than Jeanne, and I couldn't understand it because her work was quite obviously far better than mine. And yet M. Renoir said nothing to her. She was so discouraged. I had somehow imagined him to be far more of a teacher to her; but now I see that he really doesn't 'teach' much at all.

Wednesday 17th November

I began painting yesterday but made no progress this morning. We went to M. Renoir's studio, where he had just done the little redheaded model from Essoyes in a green dress playing the guitar. Her hands were beautifully painted, with delightful rose-coloured flesh. There was also one of a brown-haired woman in a light pink dress with a guitar at her side and a table with a blue vase and a nicely painted carpet; then, on a small upright canvas, the same figure dancing. The dress had a hazy, floating quality which was lovely. He has also finished his two decorative panels of nude women supporting a very beautiful ornament containing fruit. They are magnificent, but I find 'décoration' quite impossible to understand.

Monsieur Renoir told us he thought Jeanne's copy was good, but was wondering how she was planning to finish it. He said it was better to start with a simple scumble to give oneself an idea of the overall effect and then to paint the figures last of all. We visited Mme Renoir, who is leaving for Essoyes again. She was very nice to us, and Jean is sweet. She talked a great deal about the medical student Jeannie was seeing at the time. Paule believes she thinks he could perhaps marry Jeannie and would like that very much. At any rate, Paule thinks a lot about Jeannie's marriage and Jeannie thinks about Paule's.

Faivre, who should have come to see us at the Louvre, didn't appear after all. It seems he has forgotten us. Monsieur Renoir teased me, saying he would come after I had been working for a long time, in order to tell me my painting was very bad, and then I'd have to start the whole thing again.

Monsieur Renoir has been very merry since his return and jokes all the time—this proves he must be pleased with what he is doing. Jeannie was saying to him the other day that Mallarmé would only ever go to the Concerts Lamoureux. 'Goodness!' replied M. Renoir, 'Is he *still* going there? That snail, Mallarmé, he's only capable of going to the same place at the same time to do the same thing.' It was just a friendly little dig. Deep down, M. Renoir has the greatest admiration for M. Mallarmé; but painters always have to run writers down. . .

Saturday 27th November

One doesn't only meet painters at the Louvre. That is to say, one does meet painters—Helleu, for example—but men of letters also come to see us. We have had a second visit from M. Mallarmé, and one from Arsène Alexandre.

Paule has definitely started working on LA VIÈRGE AU LAPIN. I am working on my huge canvas, but it will never be finished, especially if I only add a bit every two weeks. I am filled with admiration for Jeanne's LA VIÈRGE ET L'ENFANT, which I didn't really like a few days ago.

We spent the evening at the Odéon in M. Mallarmé's box. They were giving a recital of his prose poem *Le Phénomène Futur*, which was really delightful, so charming and fine, and for which M. Renoir has made a lovely etching. They also recited other wonderful things. . . Whenever I hear some of Mallarmé's work, I find it beautiful and I have to ask myself why it's supposed to be 'incomprehensible'. I'm probably dreaming, or not attempting to fathom literature, because I really believe I understand it—I, who know nothing about it. I think writing must be one of the most difficult things to do. I wonder how on earth one makes up verses?

1897

Sunday 28th November

It's annoying when one is already feeling a bit miserable to wallow in a mire of stupidity such as we saw and heard at the Folies Bergère with Mme Renault and Berthe. We thought we'd find it very amusing, but really it was too silly. Unhealthy in every sense of the word, to spend three hours in a smoky atmosphere looking at idiotic clowns, stupid ballets, and atrocious women in pantaloons.

People take dozens of children along to see all this, children to whom they would probably not show paintings with naked women in them. Well, I find it more extraordinary to show them frightful women with plunging necklines, tightly-laced waists, and skimpy pantaloons.

In any case, I am *never* going back to the Folies Bergère. And as for Loïe Fuller [the dancer, painted by Toulouse-Lautrec and Forain], which is why we went there in the first place, I thought she was rather a disappointment. Even at the beginning I thought the colours were harsh; the suns, the stars, and moons were very ugly, though at the end there were a few pretty things.

Friday 3rd December

Monsieur Renoir came to see us at the Louvre. He gave Jeanne an excellent lesson and told her to take a section and finish it in one go. He said that Ingres always painted a torso in one go, free to begin it again the following day. He thought Paule had begun her copy very well and skilfully, but told me there were some mistakes in mine and that I should avoid doing something too big, although it was quite good and very 'pretty'. I was pleased, as I had no idea how I was getting on.

We spent a long time looking at Delacroix's FEMMES D'ALGER with M. Renoir. He remarked that when one has painted something like that, one can certainly rest on one's laurels. We went on to see all the lovely things from Pompeii and Egypt. How attractive Egyptian art is.

Sunday 5th December

Sermon at St Philippe du Roule on the Immaculate Conception. Monsieur Renoir came to dinner, preceded by the two little maids who accompany him on the round of visits on Sundays. Since Jeannie was playing a melody from a ballet, M. Renoir came in doing a dance step. He gave a great eulogy on Wyzewa; said that he really writes very well and has lots of talent. And he spoke with enthusiasm of Alexandre

Dumas, who will be read, he said, far longer than Zola (whom he despises). One of M. Renoir's principles is that art must be amusing and understandable.

Wednesday 8th December

Met M. Degas at the Louvre, who spent an hour and a half chatting to us about painting. 'What a pedantic old fool you've been listening to!' he joked.

He gave a great deal of advice to Paule about the copy she's doing, which he thought had been started very well. But what shocked him was a section of white canvas, which he wished to see covered—he said that one shouldn't try too many tones; that in the VIÈRGE AU LAPIN the fabrics and the moutains should be done with the same blue as the sky; the flesh passages and the orange fabric with the same tone. 'That's what gives a painting harmony', he said. He spoke about grounds: all the old painters painted on a dark ground; Titian with varnishes and glazes.

He looked at Jeanne's copy, which he thought was pretty but somewhat bungled. In front of mine he said: 'She has quite a knack, young Julie; the armour is skilfully done, it's stylish; but still the white canvas—one could say it runs in the family.' 'Skilful and stylish' pleased me. I'm always afraid that I lack these qualities, which I think are absolutely essential in a woman. Everything that has been said to me about my copy gives me encouragement.

Monsieur Degas showed a great deal of interest in a Miss Bauard who has been copying the same painting for the last ten years. 'She has the effect on me of an ecclesiastic in mufti', he said. 'With her great veil she looks like a Philippe de Champagne. I once told Arsène Alexandre that I had never heard her utter a syllable, so, going up to her, I made a point of commenting on a painting; but she replied so discreetly that I heard not a word.'

Monsieur Degas led us into the gallery where the Primitives are hung, to see how his pupil M. Rouart, whom he had advised to prime a canvas with green to copy a Mantegna, was getting on. Unfortunately he had done it in a really bright green.

All in the same breath, while telling us that such and such a canvas must be primed in such and such way, and showing us how often one finds the same tones in a painting, M. Degas kept repeating: 'What a pedantic old fool I am! Oh, dear me, just a pedantic old fool!'

Thursday 16th December

The dinner with Mallarmé and Renoir was very enjoyable: conversation between these two great men is always charming. Monsieur Renoir recounted, in a very droll way, how, having been invited to a wedding at Vincennes, he couldn't find it, and so went to another one which was taking place in a huge space, like the 'Salle des Pas-perdus', from which other rather smarter weddings could be glimpsed in reception rooms with walls decorated with blue skies and cupids. These wedding parties were having such a rotten time that in the end they came out of their private salons and mingled with the others to such an extent that, when it was time to go, the newly-weds could not find each other.

Saturday 18th December

Today my Tante Chevalier was buried, which made me think of sad things. All the family was gathered together; even Oncle Octave [Thomas] came. We didn't weep much for this poor old aunt—when one dies at the age of 84, it's quite natural. I had thought I was suitably attired for a funeral, but at the Louvre I attracted a certain amount of attention, and a gentleman came up to me and said: 'Mademoiselle, M. Henner has just admired your outfit.'

'That is because it's artistic', said the man in charge of the easels, who is one of the nicest to me.

Thursday 23rd December

We went to the Renoirs for dinner, where we were to have met Wyzewa though only Arsène Alexandre and Abel Faivre (who was less merry than usual) were there. Monsieur Renoir was charming and Mme Renoir as pleasant as could be. She has really taken to us since we spent so much time chatting to her about her part of the country. She was coughing a great deal, and taking only milk, and was starving hungry. She's getting thinner—or rather, less fat.

At dinner we discussed the Dreyfus Affair, which is back in the news at present and is quite extraordinary. How horrible it would be to have condemned this man if he isn't guilty—but it couldn't possibly be so. Arsène Alexandre criticized Roday for not having gone further and said the affair was far from being over and could bring about serious consequences. He appears to find the situation critical.

We all ended up laughing a great deal with Faivre, who, though really rather gross, is nevertheless funny. We treat him as a chum, and are not afraid to say silly things when he is present.

1898

On 5 January 1895 Capitaine Alfred Dreyfus, French artillery officer, having been wrongly convicted of spying, is stripped of his rank in front of the Ecole Militaire in a formal ceremony of humiliation

Saturday 8th January

I went to see M. Renoir in his studio. He's been doing more things than ever this winter and showed me a ravishing portrait of an actress from the Variétés wearing a Directoire period costume with roses and a huge grey hat. After that he started on a *loge* at the Variétés and lots of things using his maid as a model. He thought my hat was very pretty, which pleased me as I never buy a hat without wondering whether M. Renoir will like it.

He told me he's going to paint all three of us and he laughed a good deal at the story about Dr Evans, who has left part of his fortune to his native city, Philadelphia, requesting them to put up a statue in his honour costing not less than one million and not more than two.

'What on earth would they make it of?' asked M. Renoir. 'Out of rhinoceros' teeth, or perhaps with enough room inside for a dentist's consulting room?'

The very thought of a dentist wanting a statue like that is infuriating. Why couldn't he have left something to the Mallarmé family? What pleasure it would have given me to see them comfortably off at last.

Saturday 15th January

Today I was at Renoir's studio, where the Dreyfus Affair and the Jews were being discussed. 'They come to France to earn money, but if there is any fighting to be done they hide behind a tree', said M. Renoir. 'There are lot of them in the army, because the Jew likes to walk about wearing a uniform . . . They are asking that the Dreyfus Affair be made public [the original trial, in 1894, was held by a secret military court], but there are some things which simply cannot be said. People don't wish to try to understand that sort of thing,' he added.

Monsieur Renoir also let fly on the subject of Pissarro, 'a Jew', whose sons are natives of no country and who do their military service nowhere. 'It's tenacious, this Jewish race. Pissarro's wife isn't one, yet all the children are, even more so than their father.'

Thursday 20th January

Charlotte [the maid] spent two days working on this evening's dinner, as it had to be simple yet delicious and she managed to achieve this result. Unfortunately there were too few men to eat it. It would have been so successful—five men and five women.

A menu decorated by Julie Manet

Yesterday M. Mallarmé forwarded Mauclair's letter saying he couldn't go out because of bronchitis, and added that he had invited Geffroy. How embarrassing for us, as we don't know him. Today M. Faivre sent a telegram saying he had influenza. And in the end M. Mallarmé arrived without Geffroy. Geneviève had set out to please all the men she was expecting to see; M. Renoir arrived alone and we waited and waited for Arsène Alexandre.

At last, at half past seven, there was a ring at the door. 'Ah, here he is at last!', we cried. The door opened and a woman came in, so I assumed he'd brought his wife and imagined that he was pushing his wife in ahead of himself. But it was Mme de Loute, come at that hour to pay a visit (that is, to discuss the price of the dancing classes we were trying to organize).

We told her quite frankly that she had come rather late, but she made no move to leave. Finally she left, and we sat down to dinner without A. Alexandre, who never materialized. The whole thing was so aggravating that the only thing to do was to laugh about it, and, after that, we enjoyed a charming conversation between M. Mallarmé and M. Renoir.

We had two men there, when we should have had five or six, or even seven, since we had gone over to invite M. Degas, but, finding him in such a state about the Jews, we'd left without actually asking him.

At dinner we discussed the Dreyfus Affair a little. Now they're saying that Arsène Alexandre is a Jew. Monsieur Renoir talked about Zola and his way of seeing only one side of an issue and of discrediting the general public. 'It is just like a person who half opens the door of a thatched cottage, notices it smells nasty in there, and goes away without even bothering to go into the dwelling', he said. And added that, when in the past he used to go to the Moulin de la Galette, where all the working-class families of Montmartre gathered, he couldn't help noticing just how discerning were the opinions of these people of whom Zola spoke as though they were all quite atrocious.

Saturday 22nd January

Paule and I went to Durand-Ruel's where we saw the two decorative panels M. Renoir has just done, with a figure in blue playing the guitar and another in pink playing the tambourine. They're delightful. The skirts have an unparalleled lightness as they swirl on the ground and the ornamentation is very pretty, as are the charming little cupids.

We also saw pictures of a woman with a guitar with a little girl dressed in red listening to her, which is just as delightful. Monsieur Renoir has painted the fabrics, cushions, and carpets in an extraordinary manner. And I viewed with pleasure his beautifully painted nude woman with brown hair against a background of sea, and the other one with blonde hair and wide eyes, her hair lifted by a gentle breeze against a hazy background of sea and rocks.

Thursday 27th January

We went to see the Rouart Collection with the Baudots. For me it was a revelation of Corot's talent; I thought I knew him through his delicious landscapes but I didn't know quite everything. When M. Renoir talked about his figures with such enthusiasm, I was unable to share his admiration as I had never seen any of them; but Corot's great genius was made apparent to me today. Until now, though I liked him, I didn't appreciate him as he should be. Monsieur Rouart has some delicious figure studies by Corot—one in a pink dress with long thin arms, a charming one in grey, a delightful one with black bandeaux and something yellow on her head, and another marvellous one; and an astonishing drawing and some extraordinary landscapes—the l'Île de St Bartolomeo, all made up of pink buildings reflected in the water; a view of the Coliseum with superb lines of mountains, trees so rounded and of that grey peculiar to the Midi; then lots of others with willowy trees against the sky. Oh! that Corot grey, against which a ravishing and enchanting colour occasionally stands out.

After having seen all that, one thinks about it; one dreams and one thinks of all M. Renoir says about Corot.

Monsieur Rouart has, besides works by Corot, other beautiful things: a magnificent copy of L'ENLÈVEMENT DES SABINES by Poussin done by M. Degas in an even more beautiful tone than the original; then some charming dancers, again by M. Degas—they are perhaps less unusual than those Manzi has. A large painting by M. Renoir of a woman on a dappled horse and a child on a pony in the same colour—the horses embody an astonishing amount of movement, the horsewoman is full of grace, and the background is delightful. I had never seen anything by M. Renoir in that genre . . .

By Oncle Edouard, there is the LEÇON DE GUITARE (I think that is the title). It's superb, but placed very high up; the fat, short arms of the woman are astonishing. Then a very beautiful bust of a woman with a piece of velvet around her neck; and finally Tante Suzanne in one of her grey dresses (in which Oncle Edouard often painted her), sprawled out on a beach with a man next to her (M. Rouart says it's Papa but it doesn't look like him). One can see a faint line of sea, which is quite dark as it is before a storm. It's both lively and vivid.

We saw a delightful painting by Maman of a person on the terrace of a chalet, with a background of sea and a very high cliff and a little path which can be seen winding its way and becoming lost to sight little by little. It must have been done at Fécamp like the one by Oncle Edouard, before Papa and Maman's marriage. There is a beautiful marine by M. Monet; a boat seems to go forward slowly in a blue haze; also two landscapes. And a pretty thing by Delacroix, another by Fragonard, and many by Daumier.

Sunday 30th January

Monsieur Renoir came to dinner with Pierre and talked about the petition which the Jews, anarchists, and men of letters are signing at the moment for a reconsideration of the Dreyfus trial, and the fact that Natanson came to ask him to sign it. Naturally he refused and wouldn't attend a dinner given by Natanson's secret society (where he once held a discussion on the topic 'Where does the bourgeoisie begin and end? Am I a bourgeois?'—to which 'No, we are intellectuals!' was M. Renoir's reply).

Saturday 5th February

Today I went to M. Renoir's studio to say goodbye as he's leaving for the Midi tomorrow. Well at least he thinks he is, but really doesn't know what he's doing as he keeps changing his mind.

Later, we went to meet M. Mallarmé at the Odéon where he offered us seats in his box. We heard some classical poems by Leconte de Lisle recited by Mme Méry Laurent [model and mistress of Edouard Manet, Mallarmé, and the President of the Republic]. They were very beautiful. We also heard a pretty poem by Edgar Allan Poe translated by M. Mallarmé and some charming verses by Mme Desbordes-Valmore filled with feminine delicacy about roses whose petals were falling. There were a few old ones by Baudelaire which were very lovely, and a fragment of *Aphrodite* by Pierre Loüys—very sad and beautiful.

Saturday 12th February

I went to see Tante Suzanne. She is greatly preoccupied with the Zola trial. As far as she is concerned, Zola is acting in good faith but is mad. She buys the evening papers to see if someone hasn't thrown him into the Seine. It would cause her grief to know that this man whom she knew had been badly treated.

Wednesday 23rd February

I saw Oncle Edouard's JARDIN DES TUILERIES at Durand-Ruel's. How beautiful and amusing it is, and how nice all the figures are. Nearly all the men are well-known artists—there's Oncle Edouard in a corner, and Papa doffing his hat is very well painted.

Saturday 26th February

Monsieur Renoir got back this week and he came to eat oysters with us this evening. He thought that Labori defended Zola very badly. As for the latter, he never said anything about Dreyfus but spoke only about himself—about his tomes which have brought the French language to the entire world, etc.

Monday 28th February

An absolutely ghastly accident has just happened to the man who lives opposite, Colbach, who hires out carriages. His son, who has been married for a year, was out for a ride in a carriage yesterday with his wife when an electric tram ran into them. He was thrown on to the rails, broke his skull, and died last night. The poor young wife, who is in an interesting condition, had a broken wrist and swollen head. What a tragedy! This man, who had been brought up among horses, was a fine driver; to die at twenty-nine in an accident like that and leave a young wife of twenty in her state—it's horrible. Poor people!

The father, who seems such a nice person, and the sister, must be stunned. I cannot help thinking about it and would like to be able to help these unfortunates.

Wednesday 2nd March

Whenever I go to the cemetery, behind the big cyprus tree which shadows the granite tomb, I see a blue sky which seems to say to me 'Those for whom you mourn are happy'. Today despite the heavy showers while I was praying, a ray of sunshine appeared at the same time as a few patches of blue sky. Maman, Maman! Tell me if I am displeasing you. Tell me if I am taking a path which you don't approve of. I would like to have a character imbued with your own, love what you loved and would have loved, paint as you would have liked me to, in short really be your daughter. If only I could be like you. The whole of life to live through without seeing you again is a long time; I want to be worthy of seeing you again afterwards. Maman, who I loved so much, please inspire me!

Thursday 17th March

We dressed up in costumes to entertain M. Mallarmé and M. Renoir (who didn't seem to be the least bit in Lenten mood) this evening, and the interminable discussion on the Dreyfus Affair started yet again, with the same things being said once more. Monsieur Renoir said that the peculiarity of the Jews is to cause disintegration etc. (which is true). They may well be very interesting but really one has had quite enough of the whole affair by now. We three couldn't think of a thing to say.

It must have looked ludicrous to see these two men in serious discussion (one of whom, M. Renoir, was very worked up), while three people wearing costumes which were more or less ridiculous were sitting down listening to them and not opening their mouths once.

Saturday 19th March

Today I visited Durand-Ruel's where some of Oncle Edouard's superb canvases are on view at the moment. There is a TOREADOR (Oncle Gustave, I think) standing up with crossed legs against a brown background, dressed in black with a pair of admirably painted yellow boots. The black costume and cape are also well painted. The drawing of the body, squeezed into a wide pale grey and pink cummerbund, is astonishing. The hands are very lifelike, and the vermilion cape, pleated and with tassels (which look so woolly) which the toreador is wearing, is extraordinary. What a magnificent piece of painting! One can almost feel how much he weighs and one can see the quality of the wool.

What a lovely contrast with the canvas opposite, which is of a woman in a toreador's costume holding up a length of pink fabric which is so light that the slightest breeze would lift it. The hand in the fabric is beautiful and the silk stockings outlining the legs are pretty. Behind the woman dressed in black (it's the same one as in OLYMPIA, the DÉJEUNER SUR L'HERBE and other paintings) [Victorine Meurent, one of Manet's favourite models] the entire arena can be seen, with figures in the distance and a man on a horse—all done in Venetian grey and red.

What a lesson in painting it is to look at that picture! The TOREADOR is certainly one of Oncle Edouard's masterpieces. I also saw the MUSICIENS, the L'EXÉCUTION DE MAXIMILIEN, the lovely JARDIN DES TUILERIES, and the RUE DU 14 JUILLET. The painting of d'Espagnat (a young man who is having an exhibition at present), seems very coarse. There were some nice things; some still lifes, which, though pretty, were very badly painted. As for the rest—well, it's hard to hold one's own next to Oncle Edouard.

Tuesday 29th March

In the afternoon we saw the Goupil Collection, which is going to be sold tomorrow at the Hôtel Drouot. There was the 'ALABAMA', off the coast at Cherbourg with a very green sea, by Oncle Edouard (retouched), and also his painting of Tante Edma (in a white chiffon frock with a child's pram behind her) and Oncle Tiburce. There were some lovely racehorses by M. Degas, some Corots, a very nice landscape by Pissarro, quite a number by M. Monet (two of which seemed very good to me—a winter scene of grey trees against an orange sky and a summer one of some trees and houses reflected in the water).

We met M. Degas, but M. Monet had just left. We'd love to have seen him and to have had some more news about his wife's youngest son, who, while doing a chemistry experiment, burnt both his eyes. What an atrocious accident! Nothing but tragedies. Happily he can now see clearly, for it would have been terrible if he had remained completely blind. For Mme Monet to have a paralysed daughter and a blind son—what a frightful thing to happen.

Friday 22nd April

Spent the whole week sewing on petals—it's the very devil of a job making these costumes. [The cousins were going to a fancy-dress ball the following evening.]

Camille Pissarro

Saturday 23rd April

There was pressure all round, but at last everything was finished on time. We did Paule's hair, powdered her, and put on a little make-up. Her costume is nice, but I prefer her in her pink satin dress.

Tante Edma and Blanche came up to dress us. Edma and the de Loutes came to see us and even ended up helping with the final details. Our costumes seemed quite pretty when we left home, but by the end of the ball we looked like withered flowers. They weren't very successful and were too different from the others, which in general were too ornate.

Sunday 29th May

Today I read some of Maman's letters addressed to Mme [Sophie] Canat; they're quite simply lovely. I couldn't help crying when I saw how much affection Maman had for me and everything she did to contain herself in front of me after Papa's death, so as not to show her pain and to try to distract me. What a sacrifice just for me. Why, instead of not daring to talk about Papa, didn't I cry with Maman? We could have talked about him together and it would perhaps have been less hard. That's one thing with which I shall always reproach myself. Maman only had the best in mind for me—how she cherished me.

In other letters to Tante Edma she spoke about me all the time. Her style is one of delicious simplicity. Her letters are almost conversations. Ah! what a charming person Maman was, and what an artist!

Friday 3rd June

It was the opening of the Monet exhibition yesterday. Only Paule went to it. She saw the whole Monet family and Germaine was kind enough to come and see me today. She told us about the frightful accident that happened to the Helleu family yesterday. While M. Helleu was at the Monet exhibition, his youngest grand-daughter, aged 18 months, who was being taken for a ride in a little carriage, was run over by a carriage whose horses had bolted. This happened on the Avenue du Bois almost in front of the windows of the unfortunate parents. Poor people! What an atrocious thing to lose a tiny creature of 18 months like this. Their little boy was present at the catastrophe—what a ghastly impression it must have made on him. It's really a terrible piece of bad luck for such a thing to happen on the Avenue du Bois, where children are usually quite safe. It's dreadful, all the accidents that can happen. How sorry I am for the families of the victims.

Sunday 5th June

I went to Mme Quesnoy's; then on to a meeting of the *Enfants de Marie* to which, as from today, Jeannie and I belong as novices. The reception ceremony was inspiring: calm and very religious. I put myself under the protection of the Holy Virgin, asking her to look after me; and made the resolution, as a Child of Mary, to be a better Christian and to help others more. It's about time I began helping the poor and serving other people. I shall be twenty soon, so I ought to start.

Monsieur Renoir came to dinner. He wondered why the Monet exhibition had not impressed him and asked Paule what she thought of it. She replied that she had found it boring too. Then he said that he thought Pissarro's street scenes were pretty bad.

It appears that Arsène Alexandre, not knowing what to write about these two exhibitions, came to ask M. Renoir's advice.

Claude Monet *'La Barque Rose à Giverny'. Madame Hoschedé, Monet's second wife, had six children by her first husband and here we see three of her daughters in a punt on the Seine*

Renoir declared: 'Monet—quite superb!' 'Very well, then, I'll say it's superb', replied Arsène Alexandre. 'Pissarro—utter rubbish!' resumed M. Renoir. 'Oh, indeed, then I'll say it's very poor.' 'No—just say that it's less good.' Look what becomes of even the most intelligent of art critics!

We talked about the Salon [the Salon de la Nationale at the Champ-de-Mars]. Monsieur Renoir thought the Anquetin quite good; Lerolle no worse than everything else; the Puvis de Chavannes so bad that he passed it a hundred times without noticing. 'The BALZAC' [by Rodin], he said, 'makes a certain impression at first, but the impression doesn't last and on reflection one finds it less good. Sculpture which is meant to last ought to be calm.'

Monsieur Renoir was particularly interesting this evening. He told us about how he was one of the first to know Wagner's works, being a member of a society to which Lamoureux, d'Indy, etc. also belonged, as well as sharing a studio with friends who played a lot of music. Often, after he had gone to bed, he could still hear Wagner and would have to shout 'For heaven's sake! Will you be finished soon?'

About that time he went to Italy and his friends advised him to press on as far as Sicily in order to see Wagner who was at Palermo, and bring back his portrait for them.

Monsieur Renoir went there and was received by Mme Wagner, who told him that her husband could see no one as he was in the midst of finishing a score. Monsieur Renoir waited for a few days, and finally had an interview with Wagner, and in half an hour did the superb portrait which was shown in his exhibition in '92. It must look just like him. Apparently one recognizes old Wagner's piercing blue eyes when one sees the portrait.

Thursday 9th June

I went to M. Monet's exhibition, quite decided not to be influenced by what had been said to me. Contrary to the opinion of many people, I found the flowers beautiful. I thought I was seeing one of those clumps from a chrysanthemum show—those gigantic prize chrysanthemums in superb colours. His SEINE series seemed very sad to me, though two with quite choppy water appealed to me very much. I saw the beautiful cathedrals again, with yellow, golden, green tones against blue skies, and two all pink which made me think a bit of strawberry ice cream. Many views of Pourville were superb, among them one with a very blue sea and pink coastline, with a cliff throwing a shadow on to the sea, and one with a green sea frothing up on to a lilac-coloured beach.

Obviously the overall impression isn't very amusing; it rather tends towards the monotonous in the large Petit gallery (when one is called Petit, one does things on

Monet in his garden at Giverny, probably in June 1921

a large scale!) where one panel is taken up with landscapes of Norway, another by the series of Seine pictures in greys, the third by the cathedrals, and the fourth one by seascapes. There is certainly method in the whole thing.

On leaving we went to Durand-Ruel's and, to our great astonishment, on going in by the Rue Le Peletier we saw a room of smiling, happy works by M. Renoir, such as the superb DÉJEUNER À BOUGIVAL in which one always discovers something amusing, the DANSES in the country and in the town (the two white gloves of the dancer are astonishing); LA LOGE, which I like enormously; children with hair bleached by the sun against a background of sea; and torsos, and many figures. Also in the middle of these older works, delightful little studies of heads done this winter.

In the second gallery are some landscapes by M. Monet which are not at all sad: lilacs, seascapes in the Midi, and some superb olive trees. Next to these are some of Pissarro's Parisian street scenes which look as though they were done from the roof-top of a house. One can see as if looking from above great numbers of omnibuses and carriages, but the unfortunate thing is that the horses are seen in profile and always seem to be leaning to the right (how slippery the paving must be if the horses keep falling sideways). It's all black and white; in short not very successful. I remember Pissarro exhibitions with figures in the meadows, which were very pretty and nothing like this at all.

Next, another small gallery is given to Sisley, who has some delightful landscapes—nature itself. The Bougival bridge reflected in the clear water made me want to be there. Also a riverbank with a very leafy tree rising up towards the sky was extremely pretty too.

On the way out we saw a delightful dancer by M. Degas.

OPPOSITE
Alfred Sisley *'Le Pont de Moret'. Julie tells of Sisley's death in her journal, although he was not a close friend. She knew both Renoir and Monet greatly admired his work*

Alfred Sisley

Sunday 12th June

I went over both Salons and the Indépendants. It was exhausting. When one goes to the Salon du Champ-de-Mars, one knows one is not going to be impressed; but when one goes to the Champs-Elysées [the official Salon] one is utterly disgusted. Happily it is possible to forget this painting in order to think about the things at Durand-Ruel's and at home. How on earth can people know anything at all about painting by going to the Salon every year?

Thursday 16th June

After dinner we paid a short visit to M. and Mme Renoir. We were very kindly received and talked to M. Renoir about his exhibition. He told us that in LA DANSE he had used Mme Renoir and his friend Lauth (of whom he still speaks with affection).

The portrait of Jean in black velvet with a guipure lace collar and a hoop in his hand is hung in the salon. It looks very good and one could almost take it for the portrait of a little prince.

Friday 1st July

We went to M. Renoir's studio to see his panels of Grecian ladies painted to decorate doors. They're delicious—full of movement, with subtle draperies and luminous yellows.

Monsieur Renoir is leaving tomorrow for Dieppe, where he will be spending three days looking for a house for the summer, and he's offered to take us with him. To start with we said it was quite impossible—it just happens to be tomorrow that we have a meeting with our solicitor, etc. Then we thought about it, and wondered if a short break at Dieppe (with which we are not familiar) wouldn't be rather agreeable.

In the end we left M. Renoir saying that if we decided to go we would meet him at the Gare St Lazare tomorrow morning. When we got back we continued to procrastinate, and it was not until this evening that we finally sent messages and telephoned to our teachers, pupils, and the solicitor to cancel all appointments.

Saturday 2nd July

At 8 o'clock we were at the Gare St Lazare where we found M. and Mme Renoir and Jean, who fidgeted like a little devil for the entire journey and interrogated a person, who had some canaries with her, about her life, what she was going to do at Dieppe etc . . . We went past the old Meulan line, which made me think of our time at Mézy, a time so happy, alas now far away. We went through Mantes-la-Jolie and Rouen with its superb churches, but the sky was grey and the countryside not as pretty as usual.

1898

Sunday 3rd July

It was freezing at the seaside; there was no way at all of staying on the beach. When one was at a certain distance from the sea, which was really beautiful, it beckoned to you; and when you approached, it repulsed you. We went for a lovely walk on the cliff, whence one overlooks a coast which looks like those M. Monet did of Pourville. Then we went by carriage into the countryside.

The food is quite atrocious here and we are all forced to eat bread and milk. We spent the evening at M. Renoir's window looking at the landscape, the cliff cutting across the sea—that ridiculous piece of lace, as M. Renoir put it.

We were enthralled by a magnificent eclipse of the moon. It's curious to see the shadow of our earth on another planet. What a strange sensation one has when one thinks that one is on a globe. What a marvel creation is and how tiny is man in reality whereas everyone thinks himself so important . We are nothing in comparison with this immensity.

So the evening passed, at the window, looking at the moon and chatting, while the noisy sea rolling pebbles from the beach made a rumbling sound.

Monsieur Renoir didn't want to rent one of the frightful chalets here, but Mme Renoir did; so they rented one.

Sunday 24th July

We spent the day at Valvins with the Mallarmés who received us with their usual kindness, and we experienced a keen pleasure in seeing them. Monsieur Mallarmé took us for a joyful ride in his boat on the Seine. We came back to have tea in the small garden full of hollyhocks; three of them in a pretty pink colour represented us, said M. Mallarmé.

The wreck of the 'Bourgogne' [which had sunk with the loss of many lives earlier that month] was talked about and M. Mallarmé said that the captain had told Mirbeau (who had been in command of the boat which went to meet the Tzar two years ago) that he knew the sea well and that he feared one thing only, and that was the fog, because there were always Englishmen to be found there. What a forewarning!

We had dinner with a Danish lady, a friend of Geneviève's, who was very funny. She was astonished that we didn't smoke. She told us that on her arrival in Paris, out walking one day on the Buttes Chaumont with a friend, she went into a restaurant for refreshment and seeing 'absinthe' written on the menu, asked for some, not knowing what it was. 'It's not for a little miss like you', replied the waiter and brought her grenadine and water instead. After dinner we began saying our goodbyes and kissing each other. Mademoiselle (the Dane) declared that on principle she never kissed men. Monsieur Mallarmé accompanied us as far as the little station at Valvins with Geneviève and we kissed again, leaving each other with regrets and best wishes for a lovely summer.

Thursday 11th August

We left Mme Renault, with whom we have been staying since the end of July, to meet the Roudiers in Finistère at Brignogan. Life in Dinard isn't quite that of the country: I wasn't as sorry to leave the area as to leave those who had entertained us so kindly.

We stopped at Morlaix to sleep at the Hôtel de l'Europe as we did four years ago. We arrived in the evening and passed over the viaduct above the town, where several lights were shining as they had on the same day in that same year. It was with apprehension and pain in my heart that I felt the train carry me towards this place which I first saw at night and where I got off at the station and went to the same hotel where, at this very table, I saw Maman sitting, laughing that I was so pleased to be in Morlaix. Four years ago already, that last journey with Maman, which was such fun. It is my last memory of pleasure with her and I think of it often.

Monday 15th August

We went to a superb procession—never have I seen such beautiful costumes. Women in lace *coiffes* on top of golden head-pieces, wearing dresses of red and violet satin embroidered in gold, with blue lace shawls held together with jewellery and tinged pink by their transparency against the dresses, carrying reliquaries and statues of the Virgin. Little girls in dresses of white spotted muslin with huge sugar-loaf bonnets were carrying banners.

One would have thought one had been transported to another century seeing these women adorned in such riches. What superb colours; and what a subject for a painting this procession in the countryside would have made, on its way back from a calvary, with a group of thatched cottages and the sea as a backdrop.

Julie and her cousins spent the next ten days in Brittany, returning to Paris on 25th August overnight before leaving again for a holiday in Burgundy with Jeanne Baudot and her parents and the Clément family and Jacques Drogue. They all had a wonderful time, leaving the Cléments on 7th September to join Renoir at Essoyes and to begin painting again.

Mallarmé on the banks of the Seine with Paule Gobillard and Thadée Natanson
(photograph taken by Julie Manet in 1896)

Saturday 10th September

Oh! The most terrible thing has happened! A dispatch has just informed us of the death of M. Mallarmé. It cannot be possible—what could have been wrong with him? It's frightful. Poor Mme Mallarmé and poor Geneviève. How unhappy the death of this greatest friend of Papa and Maman makes me. He was so wonderful to us; he called us 'the children' in such a paternal way. He reminded me of the delightful Thursday evenings we used to have at home.

How atrocious it is to think that this man, who was looking so well in July, has now disappeared. Death is terrible.

Monsieur Renoir was greatly moved on hearing this horrible news. He's leaving with us this evening for Valvins. We are going to stay at Troyes.

Sunday 11th September

We arrived at Valvins about 2 o'clock. How dreadful it was to go down the path beside the Seine towards the small country place when we couldn't help thinking that the person for whom we were shedding tears wasn't there any more. The boat seemed to be quite solitary—his boat, the boat that he liked so much—and it reminded me of a first outing in it in '87 with Maman and Papa, who asked M. Mallarmé if he had ever written anything about his boat. 'No', he replied, casting a glance at its sail, 'for once, I am leaving this great page blank.'

My heart felt very full going into the little garden, climbing the stairs to those two unhappy women. It's horrible to see this charming interior without M. Mallarmé, and, instead of hearing him chatting in the garden under the chestnut tree which Geneviève planted when she was little, to see his coffin. It's dreadful to think that we'll never hear his gentle voice again. He had such an affectionate way of saying 'Maman' when he was talking of her to me. It is he whom Papa named as my guardian, and it was he and M. Renoir who were the two great friends of Papa and Maman. I had absolutely no idea that this winter we would enjoy their conversations together for the last time.

Both the men of letters and peasants with whom M. Mallarmé was so friendly were gathered together in great numbers in the garden to attend this funeral which was so especially heart-breaking—one could see the pain etched on every face. The ceremony at the church in Samoreau was simple and very lovely. The cemetery, where he has been laid to rest near his young son whom he lost so young, skirts the Seine and looks out on to the forest which M. Mallarmé loved so much.

Roujon, trembling, said a few words full of simplicity on behalf of the old people (Catulle Mendès, Dierx, Mars, etc.), on the personality of his friend, making all his gentleness felt. He drew tears from everyone, saying how in times of trouble in life one could always have recourse to Stéphane Mallarmé and be promised his help—'he gave you his hand of friendship, lowering his eyelids over his great child-like eyes'. What an apt and discreet portrait, just as M. Mallarmé would have wanted it to be. Paul Valéry spoke next in the name of the young people, but he was so overcome that he couldn't continue and left the cemetery in tears with Geneviève.

The day on which all one's friends come to embrace and cry with one is perhaps the least awful. What is terrible is that life resumes its normal course as though no one had gone, and, little by little, the time when you lived with the person for whom you now shed tears grows farther and farther away.

Madame Mallarmé and her daughter Geneviève in mourning after Stéphane Mallarmé's death in 1898

How dismal it was this evening after everyone had gone to find these two lonely women here. Henceforth they will be without the person they lived for. We dined with them, and in my mind's eye I could picture us all at that same table on 24th July with him. I expected at any second to see him coming in through the door with a pleasant word on his lips. Everything here is him. Valvins has lost its soul.

Monday 12th September

We slept at Mme Hubert's and will stay here until tomorrow so as not to abandon

Julie Manet *Children on a beach in Brittany. Julie spent the summer of 1895 after her mother's death with Renoir and his family in Brittany at Douarnenez*

Paule Gobillard *Julie Manet and her cousin Jeannie Gobillard in the garden at Le Mesnil*

our unhappy friend and her poor mother too quickly. What can we do to render their life less sad? I really don't know. To stay here alone is dismal; to leave these dear memories is harder still. We asked them to come to Essoyes with us, but they decided against it. I'm heart-broken and cannot understand this illness of the throat which carried off such a strong man in three days. He started feeling unwell on the Tuesday evening and died on Friday morning at 11 o'clock in the course of a frightful spasm. He had three of these crises and, after the first, he said to Geneviève: 'Could it be that I cannot live through a thing like this?' He must have felt that he was going, because Geneviève has just found an envelope in her desk on which is written: 'Instructions about my papers' but nothing was in it. Through what suffering he must have passed, what anguish thinking that he was leaving his daughter and his wife alone, and his œuvre on which he was working so hard, unfinished.

We spent the day with Mme Mallarmé, who, extraordinarily, seems almost better than usual, and Geneviève, who looks terrible. I deplore the fact that she isn't married; now it will probably be much more difficult.

Could one have predicted that M. Mallarmé would go at the age of 56? I never would have thought of his disappearance and I saw him living to a great age. What a terrible death.

Wednesday 14th September

We met M. Renoir again and talked about the poor Mallarmé family; he said some very accurate things about Geneviève's life. As he could see that we were saddened, he tried to distract us—he is really very kind with his manner of paying attention to nothing, while thinking of everything. I am becoming even more attached to him now that I have lost the other great friend of Papa and Maman. Monsieur Mallarmé and M. Renoir were the most intimate friends, the constant visitors on Thursday evenings. Ah! who is left among the habitués of those Thursday dinners? Only M. Renoir. He was there with M. Mallarmé, Tante Yves, my godfather, Papa, Maman. And out of those six people, five have disappeared in the last eight years. Only deaths!

I can't stop thinking about Geneviève and her mother and would very much like to have them here. I have been repeating Roujon's lovely words to myself and I can't help reliving that Sunday (which was yet less terrible for those unfortunate women than the days which follow: those tokens of friendship, those tears from friends mingled with their own, were less terrible than the solitude afterwards). There were very many people at the funeral, so simple and full of grief, and everyone wept sincerely—which is always friendly and good. What shocked me a great deal was not to see Mauclair who wrote a letter in which he spoke only of himself, being on holiday at Samois with a lady who was very smitten with him. He could have taken the trouble to come as M. Mallarmé liked him very much.

15th to 18th September

We sadly took up our work again. We had a model in the morning and in the afternoon painted on the riverbank. [Next day] in the morning, a study on the riverbank; in the afternoon we were in the meadows and took the bicycle out again. [On Sunday] received a letter from Geneviève, who is broken-hearted. Mme Mallarmé isn't well any more, it's distressing. We had dinner at the Renoirs.

29th September and 2nd October

Monsieur Renoir said that one must do still lifes in order to learn to paint quickly. He has just done some superb ones.

I worked on a still life of partridges on a white tablecloth with some peaches this afternoon but it's not easy. As I've vowed to work, I took my courage in both hands and went to ask M. Renoir (who is leaving tomorrow) to come and give me some advice. He gave me an excellent lesson. He said that when one begins a still life, or any other thing, one must look at the colours carefully in relation to each other and sketch very lightly, while observing closely what is black, grey and white.

'There is only black and white in painting', said M. Renoir. Then he added that one must give white its intensity by the value of what is around it, and not by putting on white. 'In the works of a great painter, the whites are beautiful and simple because he knows how to give them their place. Look at the whites of Titian, the whites of Manet, the whites of Corot' (this with regard to my tablecloth, which I didn't make stand out sufficently luminously). My partridges aren't simple enough, velvety enough; they lack colour because there are too many of them, said M. Renoir, and he added that the peaches were very good. He advised me to take it up again tomorrow and then I would see that the partridges on the tablecloth aren't right when I distance myself from the canvas.

Then he continued to talk about painting. He said that it's very good to do houses accurately, to learn to render the whiteness of walls shining in the sun. Anyway, I had a good lesson; but believe it or not, while being very pleased, I wept because I hadn't dared show M. Renoir my other still lifes and my landscapes about which I had been counting on asking his advice. Paule and Jeannie seem to find me ridiculous, and they're right. They say that this lesson on the partridges encompasses everything; that it's general and goes for all my still lifes.

Thursday 6th October

Spent all morning in the Brotel vines on the Mellet coast grape-picking and doing water-colours. The light was delicious, and the sloping vineyards enveloped with the golden vines were superb, with figures in them and sprinkled with baskets of violet grapes. Only beautiful things to paint. The scene resembled an Italian fresco, with its young girls with ruddy complexions among the vines against the background of Essoyes. How good the month of October is in the country; one especially enjoys these end-of-season marvels of nature before being shut up in Paris. Monsieur Mallarmé used to say that it was the final curtain.

Friday 7th October

I keep thinking that we are going to see M. Mallarmé on our return to Paris and it seems unbearable when I tell myself that we will never see him again.

Geneviève still writes very sad letters. She and her mother are getting better gradually. They receive a few visits from faithful friends—among them Paul Valéry who appears to be very nice. I remember that M. Mallarmé said that Valéry wished to get married and we thought of him for Jeannie. Now I've seen that he's a man of feeling, not too literary (I mean intellectual), I can imagine that he would in fact make a very nice husband for my dear Nini. But how can it be arranged? Monsieur Mallarmé once said that Valéry made him think of himself as a young man.

Saturday 8th October

Today I went for a lovely bicycle ride to a part of the Seine near a farm which was quite charming, rather like a Renoir. Saw Mussy, with its rather curious old church.

Monday 10th October

Geneviève sent us some articles about her father; some of them are very good. The one which seems to me to be the most interesting is the study by Régnier, full of awareness and truth, which appeared in the *Revue de Paris.*

Sunday 16th October

The tumult which reigns in Paris at the moment is very disquieting. I hope things don't turn out badly and am praying that it is soon over. If the railways all go out on strike there will probably be some terrible accidents. What with the strikes and the interminable Dreyfus Affair, it augurs ill.

1898

Monday 17th October

Yvonne Lerolle has told me that she's going to marry Eugène Rouart [brother of Ernest, who was to marry Julie in 1900]. The generation of which Jeannie and I are part are beginning to marry—we are most decidedly not little girls any more.

How the years fly by! In two months it will be the melancholy time of the new year. And not long after that it will be 1900, which seemed so far off when I was a child.

Thursday 20th October

Things I must look at when I go to the Louvre: Fra Angelico's COURONNEMENT DE LA VIÈRGE and whatever there is by Paolo Uccello and Filippo Lippi.

The book on the Primitives is beginning to interest me, even though it has been written in a most irritating manner. I was reading yesterday evening about the techniques of ancient painting. Fresco . . . was replaced by oil painting, discovered in the tenth century by the monk Theophilus and rediscovered by Cennino Cennini and finally by the Van Eyck brothers.

Monsieur Renoir says that he thinks true painting is done with oil rather than spirits and that one should only use that for things one wants to do more quickly. I've been trying oil for a month and find it gives greater consistency and binds better.

Monsieur Renoir is in Holland with Faivre, Durand-Ruel's son, M. Bérard, and E. We are so used to travelling that it seems very odd to me that they've gone without us. Monsieur Mallarmé laughingly used to call us the 'Flying Squadron'. I have the feeling that I've learnt something about painting here [at Essoyes] but wonder if I am imagining it?

On Monday 24th October Julie was summoned to hurry to Valvins, where Mme Mallarmé was ill and Geneviève deeply worried and upset. She stayed with them for a few days before returning to Paris. Fortunately Mme Mallarmé's illness was not serious and she soon recovered.

Wednesday 26th October

Geneviève told us the life story of Villiers de l'Isle-Adam today: his death, his marriage to a woman who couldn't even write, and the son he had by her. How very distressing it must have been for M. Mallarmé to have to insist to his friend

Julie Manet *Copy after Filippo Lippi (1406–69). This painting is known as 'Pala Barbadori' and entered the Louvre's collections in 1813*

that the marriage take place because of the child. It aroused such a sad feeling in him to see this woman sign with a cross beneath the fine signature of Villiers de l'Isle-Adam.

The newspapers are carrying very bad news about Fashoda. What a disturbing issue it is. It would be horrible to have a war with the English; their navy is so strong. The very idea breaks my heart.

We are spending the days here sewing and chatting in this red room which belongs to the person we would all like to see in it. We've been speaking of the past—to live among memories is still the sweetest thing, when one is sad.

We learned of the death of Puvis de Chavannes, who has followed his wife so closely to the tomb. The last time I saw him was at the exhibition of Maman's paintings, when he said a few words to me.

I remember in the past he would often come to the house, especially when we were at Bougival. It was there that one day, seeing him arrive, I shouted out: 'Look, it's the gingerbread man!', a name I had given him because of his red complexion. I must confess he was quite astonished by my remark—children are such terrors.

He wrote a lovely letter to Maman in '92 after her exhibition at Valadon's. A long time ago they used to correspond regularly and I have many of his letters.

Julie Manet and Jeannie Gobillard at the Mallarmés. In the foreground is Geneviève Mallarmé sitting next to her mother

Thursday 27th October

Geneviève told us of Mauclair's passion for Mlle Leblanc; how she dropped him; and how the aforesaid Mauclair had found his own passionate letters to her in Maeterlinck's house. And how he therefore took his revenge on her in the *Soleil*, using words which were mainly supplied by Mallarmé.

Geneviève is in the grip of melancholy. One feels that nothing can help her out of it. It's very distressing. She has lost both her father and her best friend. One simply cannot get used to his disappearance.

Thursday 3rd November

Visited Tante Suzanne; then went to the Renoirs (who weren't there); and finally on to M. Degas, who received us very kindly in his studio where he had just been working on a delightful tiny wax model of a nude woman. We talked about the sad Mallarmé family, and about M. Renoir and Jeanne Baudot (whose way of saying '*Bonjour*' M. Degas finds so charming).

'Her charms have seduced me', he said. Then all of a sudden cried out: 'What if I married Mamzelle Baudot? That would be an odd sort of marriage!' Monsieur Degas talks of nothing but marriage. While on the subject of Yvonne Lerolle's with Eugène Rouart, he mentioned that last winter at the Louvre he said to Ernest Rouart: 'Well, you see these young ladies—To which one do you wish me to make your request? I can assure you you will not be turned down. You are pleasant, you are well-off, and you don't appear to be too much of a rake'.

Friday 4th November

Today I went to Jeanne Baudot's studio, where we found Jeanne Clément looking charming in her grey dress and grey hat with two pink camellias against her black hair. Monsieur Renoir was there too, looking somewhat younger than usual.

We all paid a visit to Mme Clément, and made M. Degas' proposal of marriage to Jeanne Baudot. Catherine [one of the Baudot servants] declared that M. Degas is far too old for Mlle Jeanne.

Monday 14th November

Here I am, already into my twenties—twenty years old. My birthday was celebrated pleasantly at Bellevue where we went for lunch. All the children met me with flowers in their hands shouting '*Vive Julie!*' Then an excellent luncheon was served on a table covered with flowers. We drank champagne to the delight of the five charming children seated around the table, with their lovely faces—Maxime and Juliette in particular with their hair so blonde. Then they brought me a magnificent cake on which was written 'Long live Julie—14 November '78'. Everyone is so kind to me.

Wednesday 7th December

We drove Jeanne Baudot to M. Degas'. She put on her most elegant clothes to visit her admirer, but unfortunately he received her in darkness. We spoke a great deal about M. Bertrand's letter in defence of Piquart. Monsieur Degas told us that the Rouarts follow the anti-Dreyfusard meetings and that Ernest even hit a Dreyfusard once.

Thursday 22nd December

This evening we went to the party to celebrate Yvonne Lerolle's marriage contract, which took place at M. Degas'. At the entrance Ernest Rouart gave me his arm and led me in to greet Yvonne.

I was quite astonished to find Valéry there, and had only one idea in mind—that we should find an opportunity of bringing him and Jeannie together. Ever since that day when M. Mallarmé mentioned him as a possibility for Jeannie, I have been cultivating the idea and wondering how it could be brought about. Several times recently I have wanted to mention the subject to Geneviève, but I haven't seen her alone. I had the feeling this evening that Providence was offering us the chance to act.

I kept an eye on him, sometimes losing him from sight, but then he came over to talk to M. Degas who was near us. Suddenly Paule, who evidently had the same idea as I had although we hadn't said anything to each other, took the plunge and spoke to him. Shortly afterwards I saw Jeannie on Valéry's arm, going to the buffet, chatting. I felt a surge of joy and felt that there really was a chance for this first encounter to develop. Full of similar thoughts, and following Valéry and Jeannie on the arm of Ernest, I wondered whether at this charming party we were not, each of us, on the arm of the person with whom we would spend the rest of our lives . . . but nothing could be less certain, of course.

Degas at his window with an unidentified little girl

Julie (right) with Jeannie Gobillard and Paule Gobillard (seated)

Yes, I must say I liked Ernest this evening. He put his shyness aside a little, and, as we have the same tastes and live in the same milieu, could he not be the one for me? Yes—I can say that that was the idea born in me at that party.

'I have straightened Ernest out for you', M. Degas said to me. 'Now it's up to you to carry on.'

Tuesday 27th December

Yvonne's wedding. She looked lovely in white with her blonde hair, and Rouart looked wonderful with his golden hair.

Yvonne kissed us with gentleness and affection in the sacristy, where we met Valéry again. At the luncheon given by Mme Lerolle he talked to Jeannie and Paule a great deal. As for me I cultivated Ernest, to whom I had not been very nice on Thursday.

I complimented M. Lerolle on his daughters. 'They are lovely', he said tenderly. Then he added that he hoped to be at my wedding soon. I must have looked astounded as he quickly added: 'Um, of course I don't know to whom.' Could it have been hearing certain words of M. Degas the other evening which prompted him to say that to me?

1899

A bleak start to the New Year
War with England?
Julie remembers her parents
A scandal over one of Oncle Edouard's paintings
The Château du Mesnil
Julie dreams about the future
Realism—The Desfossé sale
An exhibition of Sisley's paintings
The Doria Collection—M. Renoir's poor health
The President angers the populace
Hamlet—Julie's feelings for Ernest Rouart deepen
The Choquet sale—Edgar Allan Poe
'Sentiment' in painting and music
Julie's thoughts on marriage
M. Renoir speaks about Socialism
The Dreyfus retrial
Voyage in the Midi—Julie's 21st birthday
She decides she would like to marry Ernest
A nasty row between M. Degas and M. Renoir
A violin lesson—Julie is unwell
A visit to Alexis Rouart's art collection
'Iphigénie en Tauride'

Julie Manet *Sailing-boats in the south of France*

1899

Sunday 1st January

Rain, snow, wind, atrocious weather, visits, dinner at Tante Edma's. The year started bleakly. Geneviève learnt through Valéry, who is in the War Ministry, that we are certainly going to go to war with England, and very soon.

What a portent, and a dreadful thought! It was easy to understand that Fashoda was a pretext to enter into a quarrel and that if that didn't succeed the English would find something else. Instead of talking so much about the Dreyfus Affair, the Government should occupy itself with the means of defence of our own France. What a disaster it would be should those English devils declare war on us or force us to declare it, for we cannot continue to allow ourselves to be humiliated by them. One cannot believe in this misfortune and one dares less than ever to make any plans.

Thursday 5th January

We had a visit from Général Clément and the Roudiers whom Faivre (who brought us some good chocolates) had met by chance. Nothing could be funnier than these very different personalities together. They were followed by Leconte de Lisle and the de Loutes also with bags of chocolates under their arms. It's nice to get sweets and not just from young people.

Thursday 12th January

This morning I tidied up Maman's canvases which we haven't room to hang and which are being moved to another room on the sixth floor. The sight of those beautiful colour schemes and the handsome drawings left me in a transport of admiration. It's all there—Maman's œuvre, that of a woman such as one rarely meets, whose charm is evident in everything about her: her painting, her speech, her attitudes, her looks, her tenderness. . . Ah! Maman, you live on in your canvases; but I can't help crying not to have you any more. How I would like to kiss you. At times I feel so unhappy, I want to speak to Papa, to Maman—it feels as though I am going to kiss them, and then I tell myself, no, the void is for ever, and my heart is heavy.

Saturday 28th January

Went to M. Degas to ask him to do a drawing to publish with M. Mallarmé's poetry, but needless to say he refused since it's to be published by the Dreyfusards.

Given his opinions, I can understand him a bit. He showed us the Delacroix still life he has just bought and the self-portrait by Ingres. He gave us lots of things for Jeanne Baudot, saying: 'Everyone knows my weakness for her.'

Sunday 29th January

We went to see the Pellerin Collection with Jeanne. I don't understand this man who knows nothing about painting at all and yet seems to have total adoration for Oncle Edouard's talent—of which he has some superb examples: One of Léon Leenhoff wearing velvet in front of a table covered in quantities of beautifully painted things; NANA, LA FEMME EN ESPAGNOLE COUCHÉE SUR UN CANAPÉ, which I didn't know and which is marvellous. What painting! Then LE SKATING, LE BAR, L'ARTISTE (which I like less), a FEMME NUE with which Pellerin is enchanted, and which is beautiful in fact though the background is a black which I find astonishing, and some sketches. Some little things: HOMME SUICIDÉ, moving in its reality; ÉVA GONZALÈS; and a little Spaniard next to that one, done in four brush strokes. Some charming pastels and a sketch of Maman in profile in a violet hat and a fur coat, which is exactly like her. I would dearly love to have that canvas. We saw Maman's portrait of LUCIE LÉON AU PIANO, which is really ravishing and unusual; then MAURECOURT and a FEMME EN ROSE SUR UN CANAPÉ done with back lighting, in pastel, giving an astonishing impression of light. Pellerin also owns the pretty FEMME QUI TIENT UN ENFANT (who is taking its first steps) by M. Renoir; a pretty little landscape by Sisley; and many by Monet, among others a charming one of the banks of the Seine done *en plein air*.

We came home full of enthusiasm for this collection which shows Oncle Edouard's œuvre to such advantage. What a great painter! Nothing but reality in his pictures, and how well he captured movement. All I do is think of his wonderful painting filled with simplicity; and besides, simplicity is the first requirement of beauty.

Tuesday 31st January

Monsieur Renoir is saddened by the death of Sisley, who was his companion when he was young and for whom he has kept a great affection even though he hadn't seen him since the death of Oncle Edouard.

On the subject of painting, M. Renoir repeated that one must work for short periods and rest a good deal. 'Madame Manet knew how to work admirably', he said. Jeanne Baudot says that he constantly speaks of Maman with admiration and that he finds very special words for her. Sometimes I think again of the phrase with which M. Renoir replied to M. Mallarmé when one Thursday evening, leaving the house, he was speaking of all Maman's qualities: '. . .and with all that, any other woman would find a way of being quite unbearable.'

We spent a good part of the day at M. Renoir's. What lovely things he has in his drawing-room. YVONNE ET CHRISTINE LEROLLE AU PIANO entices my eyes every time I go there.

We had the Angoulvents, de Loutes, and Lahalle to dinner, and amused ourselves during the evening by dancing, jumping, singing and behaving like babies.

Tuesday 31st January

Terrible weather prevented us from working and Jeanne Baudot from coming. We miss her very much when a day goes by without seeing her. The more one gets to know her, the more charming, intelligent, and gifted one finds her and at the same time so youthful and gay.

As we were rather despondent Paule and I took advantage of one of the days when we weren't working to take some pictures to M. Renoir, who found them quite good and cheered us up a bit. While we were talking about the P. Collection, Mme Renoir told us that the Bernheims repainted a picture by Oncle Edouard which they sold to M. Pellerin for 100,000 francs. Paule and I did not hesitate in thinking it was the background to FEMMES NUES which was redone.

Thursday 2nd February

Ysaye Pugno evening, less interesting than the others—three Grieg sonatas, it was too much. You can imagine our astonishment at seeing Jeanne Baudot, who had only left us a quarter of an hour before and who never goes to concerts. Paule stayed at home and received a visit from Jacques Blanche, who had Oncle Edouard's BAIGNEUSES with a rubbed green background and several legs. He sold it to the Bernheims this summer for Pellerin. So no more doubt about the repainted background. It's outrageous—I have a good mind to sue those horrible Bs [Bernheims].

Tuesday 7th February

I went to see Tante Suzanne to talk about Pellerin's retouched painting and to obtain her authorization to institute proceedings. I find it quite unacceptable to allow Oncle Edouard's works to be damaged in this way. But I left again, beside myself with rage. There's nothing that can be done, or said, as Tante Suzanne had written on the back of the picture that she recognized it as being the work of her husband, although she had hesitated at first, noticing several slight alterations. 'I couldn't say that it *wasn't* by my huband', she said to me with her Dutch nonchalance, 'since the women were surely by him.'

Ernest Rouart *Portrait of Julie Manet painting in the open air—probably painted after their engagement in 1899*

Thursday 9th February

We learnt yesterday of the death of Mme Monet's poor daughter Mme Butler, who had been paralysed for many years. Her burial took place today at Giverny and Paule and I went to it. We found the poor family quite stricken; they really had no idea just how ill this young woman was. Mme Monet has bronchitis and Germaine is in a horribly nervous state. For some years now these poor people have had nothing but sorrowful events.

After having left at about seven this morning, we got back at about five and found my cousin Georges at home. We were most surprised to see him in Paris. Then Drogue visited us; also Valéry (Geneviève had told us he was coming). He is very nice and does perhaps have several points in common with M. Mallarmé as a young man, as we had learned from Geneviève.

Friday 17th February

Charlotte woke us this morning with the news of Félix Faure's death. It's unbelievable, these deaths at lightning speed.

Edme [Edme Pontillon, Julie's cousin] left for Germany yesterday. Tante Edma took his departure with great courage.

Saturday 18th February

Nomination of the President of the Republic. I had a feeling that Cavaignac might be named, and was wishing it could be Méline. One cannot understand the hesitation and then his ending up by withdrawing and giving everything away to Loubet, the Dreyfusard candidate. It's horrible to have as head of state a man sullied in Panama and to think that the army is obliged to serve and defend a man who is on the side of its enemies. He can't be French if he's a Dreyfusard.

I am enraged and heart-broken for our poor country over this latest event. I wish I were a man and could demonstrate and shout slogans. It must be thrilling to engage in politics, but at the same time quite awful.

Sunday 19th February

There were a great many demonstrations yesterday evening, but unfortunately

Julie Manet *A view of the Château du Mesnil*

Julie Manet *Two decorated plates. Julie decorated a large number of porcelain plates between 1930 and 1966. These still hang in the dining-room at the Château du Mesnil*

Julie Manet *Julie's cousin Jeannie and Jeannie's daughter Agathe*

what will probably happen is that they'll shout for two days and then calm down and Loubet will remain in the presidency.

We went down to Tante Edma's, where we immersed ourselves in the papers. We bought *L'Aurore* out of curiosity. It's a disgraceful paper. Such horrors about the army should not be allowed to be written.

Friday 24th February

There was some disturbance in the streets of Paris this evening, but quite obviously they're leaving it at that, and the Dreyfusards, Panamists, Jews etc. are going to be able to govern at their leisure. Poor France!

Thursday 9th March

We called on Mme Mallarmé for a minute, where naturally enough we found Bonniot and Valéry.

We celebrated Mid-Lent by dining at Mme Baudot's, and after dinner we attempted to go on to the boulevards to throw confetti; but there was no way we could amuse ourselves—there were too many guttersnipes about.

Friday 10th March

Went to the opening of an exhibition of young painters at Durand-Ruel. It seemed to me that Maurice Denis alone is really interesting. We met lots of people— Redon, Paule's admirer, Chausson, the Lerolles, even Yvonne Rouart and her husband, Ernest Rouart, Fauché etc. . . . Nothing could be more amusing than the opening of an exhibition, where one sees all the interesting people one knows.

Saturday 11th March

We left for Le Mesnil in a thick mist. Plessis [the caretaker] had asked me to go down to check on the repairs which must be done; but the place is not yet in ruins and I am sure I shall not see Le Mesnil fall to the ground.

Towards midday the mist evaporated in the rays of a hot golden sun, permitting us to sit on the grass in front of this dear little château which evokes such emotion in me. I have scarcely lived there and yet I have memories of it. I remember our walks from Mézy to Le Mesnil when Papa and Maman were thinking of buying it; I felt it

'Le pigeonnier' in the grounds of the château at Le Mesnil, situated between Meulan and Mantes-la-Jolie

would be paradise to live in that place. And now the curious thing is that my memories are not sad but sweet ones, and I would still like to live there.

The property is most delightful and, indeed, unusual. This low château against the huge chestnut trees on the terrace, with its old courtyard, dovecote and kitchen garden, is typically French. It exudes a certain charm, which, aided by the marvellous weather, makes one want to stop time for a few moments and to sit back and dream.

How enjoyable it would be to redecorate the interior of Le Mesnil—one could do such pretty things. When will I be able to live here? Never, perhaps? One would have to come here as a family, have friends here, be married. . .

Berthe Morisot *Le Mesnil*

Monday 20th March

We had Jeanne Baudot for lunch; then I went to see Miss Vos at the Salpêtrière Hospital. She is really quite well, but she's in a state of nerves because of all the incidents happening at the hospital—disputes among the nurses, who leave the poor dying women wailing all day long without giving them their injections as they've been ordered to. Wouldn't it be better to have nuns in hospitals instead of these nurses whose interests lie elsewhere than with sick people? Nurses who on operating days think of nothing but curling their hair and adorning themselves in order to please the interns and flirt with them? Some really dreadful things go on, but little by little everyone gets used to them.

Julie Manet *Jeannie Gobillard at the piano*

Saturday 22nd April

Monsieur Renoir came to have lunch with us. He was very pleasant and quite cheerful and said it gave him pleasure to be at our house. He has a lovely way with conversation. He told us how, at the time when Courbet was making it fashionable to paint kitchens and everyday subjects [in short, the advent of Realism], Corot used to say: 'That doesn't prevent me from putting a few little godesses into my landscapes.'

I told M. Renoir that I had met Pellerin, who had urged me to come and see his new Manets (which hadn't been seen by anyone so far). 'You should have told him that even Manet himself hasn't seen them yet', retorted M. Renoir.

We next talked about Sisley, of the exceedingly withdrawn way in which he lived during his last few years at Moret, believing that everyone bore him ill-will. When he met M. Renoir with whom he had once lived, he crossed the road so as not to speak to him. He made himself very unhappy. Monsieur Renoir reminded me that, when I went to Valvins with Maman, we met him one day as we were visiting Moret. Maman invited him to come and see her at Valvins. He accepted; then, having said goodbye, he ran after her, saying: 'No, I won't come and see you after all!'

Paule showed M. Renoir the portrait of me in my red velvet dress she had just done and I showed my one of Jeannie at the piano with Paule listening to her. He gave us a few tips, such as to redo certain little bits. Monsieur Renoir is really rather encouraging.

Altogether a most delicious day with M. Renoir, who stayed until 5 o'clock. Seeing him here gave me great pleasure as he hadn't visited for such a long time.

In the evening, we went to the Opéra with Blanche to hear the *Walkyrie*. I was absolutely enthralled and captivated by this wonderful, engaging music. It's probably because I don't understand a thing about Wagner that I find the opera itself quite straightforward. In any case hearing it gave me great pleasure, and that's all I ask.

The whole day was really very pleasant indeed.

Tuesday 25th April

We went to the Hôtel Desfossé to see the collection of paintings which are to be sold tomorrow. Among them were the TOILETTE by Corot, which is very pretty, and L'ATELIER—quite delicious; as well as other Corots; Delacroix's MISE AU TOMBEAU, which is magnificent, even poignant; some beautiful river landscapes by Monet; a pretty garden scene by Renoir; a rather curious Manet watercolour painted after the PETITS CAVALIERS by Velazquez; and some Courbets, among which was L'ATELIER, which I didn't find very interesting.

*Ernest Rouart, son of
Henri Rouart and pupil
of Degas, who married
Julie in 1900*

*Julie Manet at a window
of her apartment in
the Rue de Villejust*

We met M. Degas there. While I was attentively looking at the admirable Delacroix,
he took me by the arm, saying: 'Here's a young man for you to marry!' I turned
round and saw Ernest Rouart, and we both laughed. What an intimidating way to
be introduced to someone!

Thursday 27th April

We had Geneviève with us for most of the day, which was lovely; then Mme Redon
came to see us for the first time. Valéry arrived, since he's becoming a Thursday
'regular'.

He must have been rather embarrassed to see Geneviève here because a few days
ago, when he was talking about marriage, she asked him if he was thinking of one
of her three girlfriends. 'Yes', he replied.

Jeannie seems to think he's quite nice—how I wish it would all work out.

Saturday 29th April

There was an exhibition of the paintings which were left in Sisley's studio and which are to be sold for his children, with others donated by various artists. Monsieur Monet, who is organizing it, asked me for one of Maman's canvases, and I gave him one (as Maman would certainly have done in aid of the children of an artist who exhibited with her for so long). It was a small picture of a woman in profile wearing a straw hat and went well with the other paintings.

We met M. Monet, then Germaine Hoschedé [his step-daughter], and noticed Madame Monet, who seemed to be in a nervous, morbid state. The only thing she spoke to me about was the death of her daughter.

Sunday 30th April

We went to the opening of the Salon, where we met Jacques Drogue again. He

Henri Rouart, Julie Manet's father-in-law, the painter and celebrated art collector. He was rather disdained as a painter by the Impressionists, who considered him too academic

propelled us so rapidly along in front of the paintings, to prevent us from seeing his effort, that we didn't see anything at all.

Rodin's EVE is beautiful.

We met Miss Cassatt, the Baudots, the Cléments, and Ernest Rouart (whose painting we searched for in vain).

Monday 1st May

The Sisley sale: The prices for the Sisleys went quite high, with M. Monet pushing them up. One could see that he had really taken the sale to heart and was dealing with it very seriously. Maman's painting was bought by Durand-Ruel for 3,200 francs.

Saturday 6th May

We went to the Petit Gallery to see the Doria Collection drawings; there were some curious Corots, Delacroix and Baryes. We met the Rouart family again. Ernest is very nice and I would like to get to know him well. I really wanted to talk to him today, but I didn't dare to.

I got the feeling that Paule was making fun of me. But I have no idea why, as I would have thought she'd have been in favour of it.

I don't think I was very nice to him, but I was afraid of annoying him. Oh, if only I appealed to him! I'll never see him again now, will I?

Sunday 7th May

Tante Edma took us to see Jacques Blanche. His painting is very nice and so is he. [He showed us his collection by other artists] but it occurred to us before we left that it would be thoughful to ask if we could see his own work. In all honesty we were able to make him some very sincere compliments on his still lifes.

Saturday 20th May

We went to Geneviève's. She's arranging a luncheon party at home on Monday for Valéry. She's so kind in the way she has taken this affair to heart and one can see that she wants things to work out as much as Paule and I do.

1899

Sunday 21st May

Pentecost—I took Communion at the 8 o'clock mass and prayed to the Holy Ghost. There's something I am concerned about. It is because I haven't been confirmed and I am getting more anxious as time goes on. In Mézy, which is such a tiny place, the Bishop was only able to come once every three years and, as it happened, the year I took my first Holy Communion and the one when I renewed my vows, he didn't visit. Then when we were in Paris I didn't have sufficient resolution to ask my parents if I could be confirmed. I think about this every day and will have to speak to my Father-Confessor about it.

Monday 22nd May

The luncheon with Mme Mallarmé, Geneviève and Valéry went very well. Valéry went on to the balcony to smoke and Jeannie stayed out there with him, chatting. He seems to think she's quite witty by the way he laughs at whatever she says.

He spoke rather amusingly about de Heredia, whose youngest daughter is to marry his friend Pierre Loüys, and he told us a few anecdotes about each of them. Jeannie played Schumann's *Humoresque* with unexpected charm. Valéry seemed not to dare to compliment her and Jeannie was rather annoyed by his lack of interest.

Wednesday 24th May

We went to see if Mme Mallarmé wasn't too tired after her outing on Monday; then we went to visit M. Renoir, who is in better spirits these days but nevertheless he's changed. He has decided to look after himself in his own way and to take a tonic and keep warm instead of weakening himself with a diet which forbids everything. He was working a little in his studio today, doing a pretty woman in a blouse. We also popped in to see M. Degas.

Monday 5th June

We learnt through the newspapers about yesterday when, at Auteuil, Loubet was booed, had eggs thrown at him, and was hit with a walking-stick. At last the whole populace has risen up against this unworthy representative of the State. In the Dreyfusard papers such as the *Figaro*, for example, they said that only the aristocracy were shouting and that it was a Monarchist plot. To add support to this fiction the Government released every person who had been arrested except members of the nobility.

To be President of the Republic and be the butt of insults from the very people one is supposed to be representing must be frightfully disagreeable, but Loubet is just like his friends the Jews. He puts up with insults and will never resign. If he had had to, he would have needed to wait no longer than an hour after his election.

Jacques Cor was sweet enough to offer both ourselves and Jeanne (who has been in Paris for the last week) as well as Blanche, a box at the Théâtre Sarah Bernhardt to see *Hamlet*. He also got one for the Roudiers and his sister.

In a box near us were the de Régniers, de Heredias and the Loüys family. We had a wonderful evening. There is simply nothing better than Shakespeare—*Hamlet* is quite sublime.

Wit, subtlety, tragedy, philosophy, and morals are all there and Shoeb's translation was marvellous. It doesn't seem possible that the play could have more force and charm in English. Sarah Bernhardt, playing the rôle of Hamlet, was much better than I had ever thought she could be, and I liked her more than in *Phèdre*, which was the only other time I had seen her. I was expecting to find her quite ridiculous; well, she wasn't at all. Her voice, which was rather gruff, was something of a shock at first, but one became used to it. Her appearance, movement, and agility were quite astonishing. Her mistake is to surround herself with the most pitiable actresses so as to shine even more herself.

Tuesday 6th June

We had dinner with M. Degas. On our arrival only Jeanne Baudot was there; then Ernest and Louis Rouart came. We all had a look at Post's collection, in which are some very good Forain drawings; and then it was M. Degas' turn to join us.

We went into the dining-room soon after. Monsieur Degas gave his arm to Paule, Louis to Jeannie, and Ernest hesitated between Jeanne and me, then muttered 'Oh dear, what a decision!'—and came towards me. I sat next to him at dinner and we talked quite a lot. He told me that he had been at Autun on the day of the St Ladre fair. I asked if he went to visit his brother at Autun every year and he replied that he went there last year to shoot and would be going back this year, which was what I wanted to know. The meal was a very gay affair. Ernest made himself useful, carving first a leg of lamb, then a chicken, and making coffee. After his dinner M. Degas took lime-blossom tea which he shared with Jeanne Baudot, who promised to send him some more from her garden. Monsieur Degas spoke to her about their proposed domestic arrangements, but it transpired that she likes duck not chicken, whereas he likes chicken and not duck. We told them it would never work.

During the evening we talked about the 'Affair'. The Rouarts said that Quesnay de Beurrepain speaks well. They went to a meeting for the acquittal of Deroulède. It's marvellous to see such patriotic young people; they should all be like that, but unfortunately many of them don't care about their country, France.

Before leaving we went down to see the museum; there Ernest lit the lamp to light the paintings. How well mannered he is—I can hardly help complimenting him on the way he is continually helping others. He is wonderful, wonderful. What a handsome beard! What dark eyes! I have finally managed to speak to him—he's not a bit shy, as he was when we met him at the Louvre last year, and I am extremely pleased to have made his acquaintance. I really like him, yes I really do. On the way home, in an open carriage, I thought about it all and told myself that Ernest is the one for me. . .

Thursday 22nd June

Poincaré, the minister who was supposed to re-group with Waldeck-Rousseau, finally did so today. It was nonetheless only a small task to coerce a minister to acquit Dreyfus, who is soon to be set free amid loud applause. It's disgusting to have an anti-patriotic government. They want people to believe that the Republic is under threat from the Monarchist party, but those Orléanists are half asleep and couldn't do anything even if they tried. It's the government itself which is attacking the Republic. There's no liberty any longer, one can't shout 'Long live the Army', only 'Long live Loubet and Dreyfus'.

During the course of the next few days Julie visited M. Renoir at Saint–Cloud and she went to the Salon with Paule but was disappointed by the poor quality of the paintings on view, deciding that the only decent thing was a mural by Maurice Denis intended for Vésinet College.

The Choquet Collection, on view at the Petit Gallery, struck Julie as being one of the most beautiful she had ever seen, with works by Cézanne, Manet, Delacroix, Pissarro, Renoir, and Morisot among others. Julie spent two days examining the collection, and decided to buy a small sketch by Delacroix, if she could acquire it for not more than 100 francs.

Saturday 1st July

The Choquet sale: I was very excited at the prospect of perhaps buying a Delacroix. Paule and I went to the saleroom early and asked Vollard to bid for the sketch for me.

We followed the sale with Fauché and saw M. Degas from afar looking very comical in the way he examined each item through his magnifying glass. He was sitting next to the Rouarts. I was quite emotional when Maman's painting came up for sale, but was quickly reassured when the price went straight up to 8,000 francs and finally stopped at 10,100.

The Renoirs did well, as did the Monets and the Cézannes, thanks to Vollard; but not the Manets, which was surprising. The Delacroix paintings went for practically nothing. OVIDE CHEZ LES SCYTHES, which I thought was so wonderful, only made 1,800 francs whereas I had been expecting it to go for thousands. I'm almost sorry I didn't risk bidding for it; it would have been worth having a fling. Still I was pleased as in the end I got the little sketch for 460 francs.

After the sale we went over to join M. Degas and the Rouarts. Ernest immediately asked me if I had bought anything and we talked about the prices in the sale. He said that if he could have bought OVIDE he would have done so. We discussed Renoir's portrait of Choquet, which Ernest thought very handsome. He was talkative today and joked that since he was carrying LA BATAILLE DE NANCY [bought by Degas] he would make me a present of it. I stayed behind to talk to him when everyone left the saleroom, and think we really make rather a good couple.

Monsieur Degas invited us to go to his house with him in his carriage, with the Delacroix, so we took our leave of the Rouarts. M. Degas was very sorry not to have got the Choquet portrait—'the portrait of one madman by another', as he said. He liked it enormously. Durand-Ruel bought it for only 3,500 but M. Degas had been afraid that Camondo would get it.

Zoë didn't seem in the least surprised to see M. Degas coming back with paintings. 'Since Monsieur told me he would be coming back to change, I was expecting him to bring back some pictures.' We studied the Delacroix—the one from the Desfossé sale is still the most poignant.

Monsieur Degas was an absolute darling. He discussed painting with us, then suddenly said, 'I'm going to show you some veritable orgies of colour that I'm doing at the moment', and showed us up to his studio. We were very touched as he never shows anyone what he's working on. He got out three pastels of women in Russian costumes with flowers in their hair, pearl necklaces, skirts in bright colours and red boots, dancing in an imaginary landscape that looked most realistic.

Monsieur Degas asked us which of the three looked the best; then showed us some torsos and dancers, all of which must pay for his purchases of paintings.

We left him at half past nine after having spent a truly delightful day, the sort of day that comes once in a blue moon. He arranged to meet us at the sale of drawings [on Monday]. I'd love to begin our little party all over again.

1899

Monday 3rd July

The Choquet sale: we met M. Degas who was already there; next to him were Alexis Rouart and Ernest; also the Fauchés. Mme Baudot and Jeanne (who was in quite a state because she wanted to buy something) were there too. Jeanne had asked everybody and nobody to bid for her, mixed up the lot numbers, and if M. Degas hadn't been kind enough to bid for a magnificent Delacroix watercolour for her she would have left with nothing. It was the MORT DE CAVALIER which went for 260 francs. Some of them were sold for a great deal, needless to say the very ones I wanted. Ernest seemed to be amused by Jeanne Baudot's nervous behaviour and laughed a good deal. He was just in front of me facing sideways, so I could gaze at him without any problem, and from time to time we exchanged remarks. I like him such a lot—he's wonderful. There won't be another chance of meeting now. All I can hope for is that he'll be at Autun the day we go to visit Yvonne (if we do), although he did say he was going shooting in Burgundy.

There was nothing funnier than the heirs at the Choquet sale—they are from the market district of Paris and acted as though they had never even set foot inside a proper house before: they were all there sitting on a bench, carefully marking down the price of each item in case they were cheated.

Saturday 8th July

We went to St Cloud for dinner. Monsieur Renoir looked very well and was wearing a white hat, which suited him. We dined with Wyzewa, who was charming, and his wife, who's lovely, as well as the Fauchés and Vollard, who never stopped telling anecdotes while devouring everything in sight. We all laughed when Vollard told us that he had bought Queen Christina's wardrobe at the Choquet sale and that when he had opened the door he had thought he could hear the rustle of the Queen's silk dresses.

Sunday 23rd July

Stayed at home all day; then went to the de Loutes for dinner, where we quite enjoyed ourselves. Going there is like nothing else I can think of. We drove home at midnight under the most superb moon. I went out on to the balcony for a breath of air in the light of this enigmatic and enticing heavenly body. There's a curious story by Edgar Poe about a voyage to the moon which is almost believable because of the author's vivid style.

Julie Manet *Portrait of Jeanne Baudot, painted during a trip to Brittany*

Monday 24th July

Recently I've been reading Edgar Poe's extraordinary stories translated by Baudelaire which Valéry lent us. They're beautiful, full of life; one can feel each event as it takes place and the philosophical parts are so interesting. Nothing grips me more than the sort of literature that makes me *think*; I'm fond of philosophy though it demands a certain concentration.

These horrible stories are quite marvellous. 'The Murders in the Rue Morgue', 'The Black Cat', and what about 'The Tell-Tale Heart', which is so frightening and really gives you a shock—strange tales that capture one's attention and lead to flights of fancy.

Thursday 27th July

At the Baudots at Louveciennes since Tuesday. We had a conversation on the subject of sentiment in art. I began by surprising Drogue by saying that as far as I was concerned the word 'sentiment' was the expression of everything that irritated me, and Jeanne Baudot and I agreed completely with one another on this point, holding that sentiment in painting is perfectly ridiculous, as well as in poetry and music.

Jeannie, on the contrary, said there must be sentiment in poetry and in music, that Wagner was full of it. But I, who am not capable of understanding anything whatever about music, feel that it is to impoverish the talent and genius of Wagner to apply this word 'sentiment' to him. His art is pure passion to me and I think sentiment takes away the grandeur from art which should have within itself its own sentiment without needing to have recourse to the sentimental in portraying human sensations. To say of a great artist that he has sentiment is to debase his talent. Perhaps I am taking this word the wrong way, because, as Jeannie pointed out, the painter experiences sensations and it is obvious that one must feel in order to be an artist.

I continued the argument late into the evening with Jeannie and ever more obstinately I tried to banish sentiment from art, really by contradiction, because fundamentally I think that there is no art without a certain amount of sentiment. However, as I am thought of as rather chilly, I maintain that attitude every time a discussion is brought up on a similar subject.

They think that I don't understand sentiment in anything. Take love—they think I wouldn't mind being a spinster, that I have a hatred of marriage, and obviously I let them believe all this. Sometimes I wish I could come out of myself a little, but I think that it would make Jeannie and Paule think that I don't like my life with them if I expressed the slightest idea of getting married, and yet isn't it quite natural to want what everyone surely wants? The thought of remaining a spinster is dreadful. Still, I musn't complain if that is my fate, since I have an occupation—painting— which I love so much. I have the means to pay for a few pleasures, buy pictures etc. . . . but how much nicer it would be to use what one has to bring up a family.

I am totally in favour of marriage and desire it fervently for my cousins. When I listen to them saying they were made for it, when Jeannie talks about the happiness it gives her to be loved, I want to reply that they aren't the only ones. But I keep my demeanour of being an unresponsive person who doesn't understand. Oh! but I think I do understand the enormous charm of being loved, of loving, of being looked after by a man to whom one has given oneself entirely.

Perhaps I am against marriage because I won't tolerate arranged marriages uniting two beings who don't understand each other, don't know each other, and afterwards don't get on. With divorce, marriage has lost its importance—which I find odious. For me it's absolutely sacred.

Friday 28th July

We went to St Germain this morning with Jeanne who had only one idea in her head and that was to go and see Maurice Denis, which we had never done before and we didn't know how to go about it at all. However, Paule went in to a framer's shop and asked for his address and we got as far as the door of his house.

Julie after her marriage

Later we left the Baudots to go and spend a few days with M. Renoir who is without his wife and children at the moment. He looked quite well and is possibly a bit better. He spoke about socialism, which does so much harm: 'It has taken everything away from the people, from the workers. Religion, which for them was such a consolation, has been replaced by an extra 25 centimes a day. It's not by making the labourer work fewer hours a day that you will make him happy, because a man without work gets up to no good and the labourer will spend his free time in a bar. What is needed is to get him to do work which is less taxing. There is no longer anything of interest for the working man to do. In the olden days he would make a chair after his own fashion, and with pleasure; now, one makes the legs, another the arms, and a third puts the whole thing together. They want to do the job in the fastest time possible so they can be paid. Before, a painter painted with care a Virgin who took him to heaven; now he chucks the paint at her to get her finished more quickly.'

31st July and 1st August

Monsieur Renoir continued with my portrait, which is very nice. 'People don't understand that what is hidden and has to be guessed is what gives a thing its charm', said he. 'That's why Arab women, who only allow one to see their eyes and seem so pretty, would be far less so if they removed their veils.'

Wednesday 2nd August

Everyone was in town today. Arsène Alexandre, Vollard, and M. Renoir's nephew came for dinner. We talked about Gustave Moreau. Arsène Alexandre, who wrote the most eulogistic article on him at the time of his death, wanted to defend him, saying that the things in his house were nothing like the things on view in the Luxembourg.

'It's art for Jews', concluded M. Renoir. What an apt definition of Moreau's painting!

Friday 4th August

Monsieur Renoir's health changes every day. Sometimes he seems to be fine, then his feet or his hands swell up [with rheumatoid arthritis]. The illness is aggravating for him and yet he, so highly strung, puts up with it very patiently. He is jolly, kind to us, and talks so interestingly. What intelligence! He sees things clearly as they are, just as he does in his art.

'Instruction is the downfall of the people', he told us. 'Look at these people who don't believe in the good Lord any more and for whom there is nothing left but science.' (Here again is the same idea expressed by Edgar Poe, who said that science was the downfall of mankind.)

Monsieur Renoir laughs at people who imagine that the masters of the past painted differently. He said that Geffroy concluded an article on Corot's centenary exhibition by saying, 'This is the art of the past; now we are going to see the art of the future', alluding to the Impressionists. 'So I', said M. Renoir, 'told Alexandre to write that Corot's painting was also the art of the future in his article.'

Monday 7th August

Today saw the start of the retrial of Dreyfus by court-martial at Rennes. So these Dreyfusards are going to get their revision of sentence, the only result of which will be even more trouble for our poor country. How powerful these Jews are!

Wednesday 9th August

Monsieur Renoir's older brother came for lunch and we talked about Aix—Renoir wants to have done with his treatment there, taking the waters, as he does not believe in it. He's only going to avoid being reproached for not having followed the advice given him.

'If the treatment is too irritating, I'll make Gabrielle take it', he told us, for he is taking Gabrielle with him while Mme Renoir stays peacefully at Essoyes. We all recommended him to be careful and not to tire himself out too much. It's often said that the waters do more harm than good, but if they could relieve the congestion in his hands and feet it would be excellent. It's so awful to see him in the morning, not even having the strength to turn a doorhandle.

Thursday 10th August

We went to the museum at Versailles to look at the Nattier paintings; some of them are very pretty. Next we visited Madeleine Matter, and on the way back we saw M. Renoir leaving in a little carriage towed along behind a steam-driven tricycle. He was off to have dinner with M. Degas at Durand-Ruel's but didn't look very happy with the method of transport.

As for us, when we got back Vollard arrived and we didn't dare not invite him to dinner. It must have looked very funny to see the three of us tête-à-tête with Vollard. Monsieur Renoir came back at half past eleven in a very jolly mood and we were obliged to ask Vollard to leave.

On Saturday 12th August Julie and her cousins said goodbye to M. Renoir (who was to leave the following day for his treatment at Aix) and went to stay with Mme Baudot and Jeanne at

Louveciennes for a week, before returning to Paris. The political situation was fairly turbulent, with the Dreyfus retrial under way, and Jules Guérin, co-leader of the Anti-Jewish extremists, under siege in a house in the Rue Chabrol with forty members of the League of Patriots.

On 22nd August the three cousins set off once more, visiting Mme Mallarmé and Geneviève at Valvins before going on to Givry, where they had rented a small house near the home of Général and Mme Clément.

On an expedition to Givry in Burgundy to visit Général Clément and his wife, parents of Jeanne Clément and uncle and aunt to Julie's friend Jeanne Baudot, from left to right: Jeannie Gobillard, Julie, Jeannie Clément, Jacques Drogue, and friends

Saturday 2nd September

We were woken this morning by a telegram from Yvonne Rouart inviting us to have lunch and dinner with her on Sunday at Plaines. I had written to her during the week to ask if we could come some time this month and she replied straight away. We'll have to leave for Autun tonight if we're to be there for lunch. We're finding this little 'escapade' quite amusing—tomorrow is the opening of the shooting season and Ernest Rouart told me that he would be going shooting in Burgundy. So he just might be at Plaines. Accordingly, we have accepted the invitation.

Sunday 3rd September

We went to High Mass at Autun; then on by carriage to the farm at Plaines. Yvonne was there, dressed in white. Her husband and Ernest (for he was there) were out shooting, so we went to meet them on the road; then had luncheon. We talked about M. Degas, M. Renoir, painting, literature, Valéry, Mauclair, and after lunch Jeannie played for us.

In the evening we all met again for dinner. Eugène Rouart announced that he'd like to meet Mlle Baudot, about whom he has heard so much. Since Jeannie wanted to meet Bonnard she said she'd introduce Jeanne Baudot if he would introduce her to Bonnard. We left about 10 o'clock for Autun after having spent a very pleasant day.

Monday 4th September

We woke up at half past six, and went shopping in Autun for a few comestibles that Yvonne didn't have, as we were going for a picnic at the Château de Moyeux. At nine Yvonne and Ernest came to fetch us—Eugène couldn't come. Ernest drove and I climbed in beside him 'lightly', as he put it, and off we went.

Arriving in front of the château, we could see long ranges of mountains, which Ernest likened to a Poussinesque landscape. We have discussed painting together and he has told me that he doesn't work *en plein air*—in this respect, he is most certainly a disciple of M. Degas.

Sunday 10th September

Dreyfus has again been condemned! Ten years of solitary confinement. Two out of the seven members of the Council of War voted for his acquittal. Madame Clément had written to one of her friends, a young man, asking him to telegraph the outcome as soon as possible putting 'Alphonse' for an acquittal and 'Charles' for condemned. The telegram arrived this morning, and read 'Charles: 5, 2 against'.

Monday 11th September

The Dreyfusard newspapers are furious. Clemenceau is disgusting. Gip has written an amusing article in the *Libre Parole* and Cassagnac another in *L'Autorité*, which is serious and well written.

1899

On 19th September Waldeck-Rousseau's government quashed the sentence of the Rennes court-martial on Dreyfus and conferred a full pardon (though not, as his supporters wanted, a proclamation of innocence and reinstatement in the French army—that was to come later). On 20th September Julie wrote in her diary that she was sending 6 francs to 'La Libre Parole' towards a fund for the repatriation of Jews to Jerusalem.

Saturday 30th September

We gave a luncheon party with eight places laid for four young men and four young ladies. The stronger sex would have been too few in number with only Jacques Drogue and Robert Faure-Beaulieu [godson of Mme Clément] present, so Jeanne Baudot and Mlle Ritter, in men's clothing, under the assumed names of Chevalier Gaëtan des Effluves and Baron Guy de la Hutte, both of them very rowdy, filled their roles as enterprising young men most admirably. Jeanne B. was very funny; she retained not the slightest hint of femininity.

After the meal we took photographs; the new consorts in ludicrous, sentimental poses with Jeanne C. [Clément], Paule and Jeannie; me with Faure-Beaulieu and Drogue dressed up as a woman etc. . . . We all then went off to Doyenné and then to the station to see the Baudots off. Everyone sorely missed the gay Gaëtan.

From Givry the three cousins set off on a tour of the Midi, travelling to Lyon, then down the Rhône by boat to Avignon, where they arrived on 12th October. They stayed there for three days, at the Hôtel Crillon, visiting the Palais des Papes and other sights, making sorties to villages in the area, and painting and sketching.

From there they travelled to Arles, Marseille, l'Estaque, the Côte d'Azur including Cimiez where Julie and her parents had spent an entire winter (1888–9) in the Villa Ratti which they had rented. Then Cagnes, Menton, Nice, Grasse, Aix, Nîmes, Clermont-Ferrand on 7th November, and back to Paris.

Tuesday 14th November

Twenty-one today. I had hardly even thought about it and wasn't the least bit sad at the prospect, although I gather that young ladies are supposed to take coming-of-age rather badly. Still, Jeannie cried on my behalf and that was good enough for me. I entered into my majority at Bellevue, where they had very sweetly invited people for luncheon to fête me, and everyone drank my health.

Poor Mme Guastalla, who has just been operated on for a cataract, and whose profile beneath a green eye-shade appeared even more Jewish than ever, made the wish that I would find a handsome young man. (Ugly though she may be, she worships beauty.) After hearing this my thoughts strayed in the direction of vain hopes, and I pictured Ernest as the handsome young man. I no longer have the

Julie and friends at Givry in Burgundy while staying with a cousin of Jeanne Baudot's. Julie is second from the left; then Jeannie and Paule Gobillard (the latter pretending to be a seamstress); behind her; Jacques Drogue; next to Paule, Jeanne Baudot disguised as a man and Jeanne's cousin Jeanne Clément

slightest hesitation in telling myself that he is definitely the one I would like to marry.

16th and 18th November

We had various visitors. In the evening we went to see the Lerolles, who had invited us to come and see Yvonne who is in Paris at present. At their house we met the Bernards, the Renoirs, and Ernest Rouart, with whom we chatted about the Midi and other topics. (I had a vague feeling we would see him there.)

Yvonne told us about the row between M. Degas and M. Renoir. What a shame to hear that these close friends are quarrelling. I think that M. Degas went a bit too far by writing an insolent letter to M. Renoir just because he sold one of his pastels. Even though they have argued dozens of times it seems to be quite serious on this occasion, whereas before it was never in earnest. Indeed I even remember them making things up during the Thursday evening dinners at our house.

Geneviève has lent us Boissière's book *Les Fumeurs d'Opium*, which is very interesting as an analysis of the state of someone's mind under the influence of opium and is well written too.

Monday 27th November

I went to Asnières for a violin lesson with Jules and was amazed to see he'd grown a beard. He didn't look well and was very half-hearted about everything. (He didn't seem too impressed with my playing either.)

I called in at M. Renoir's studio to say hello. He seemed to be well, and is able to work at the moment. From there I rejoined Paule and Jeannie at Mme Heude's house and we went to Mme Mayniel's for dinner, where we had one of Loubet's pheasants.

Wednesday 29th November

We went to visit M. Degas and found him, as usual, in his darkened studio, where he has a nap after working. We chattered non-stop in order to prevent him from saying anything about M. Renoir and thankfully he didn't bring up the subject, which makes me think that he probably regrets having sent the letter. He showed us a portrait of himself as a child, which still looks astonishingly like him, as well as one of his recent acquisitions—a Corot of the PONT DE POISSY which is superb.

Ernest Rouart *'At the races'.*
This painting by Julie's future husband shows his admiration for the work of his master, Degas

Friday 8th December

It has suddenly become very cold and during a visit to Valentin Scheffer I stupidly fainted while listening to an account of an accident which had befallen him. I was put into a carriage, but at home I continued to lose consciousness for a further two hours. I kept having the strangest sensations, such as a paralysed hand and fingers. I thought I was going completely crazy and imagined I was leaving Doctor Goudron de Roc's hospital. I couldn't form a sentence and didn't know what anything meant. I blamed it on my brain, which I racked in vain thinking I would never again be able to speak, and went through the most ghastly sensations, which hurt my head most dreadfully. Paule and Jeannie thought I had had a stroke and were terribly worried. When I began to feel a bit more like myself, I saw Dr Martin while Tante Edma and her daughters stayed in my bedroom.

Tuesday 12th December

We went to visit Alexis Rouart's collection with Mme Renault and Berthe. Entering the salon we saw Ernest, who showed his uncle's paintings to us, among which were some lovely Degas dancers and milliners; Corots—one of Chartres Cathedral, two landscapes and a charming figure study; some Delacroix flowers; Japanese things, etc. . .

Going up the staircase was a set of plates decorated with jockeys, singers from the *cafés concerts*, and dancers by M. Degas. I stayed looking at them for ages with Ernest while the others went into a room filled with glass cases containing Tanagra statuettes and Chinese vases, which left me quite cold. So we chatted while admiring the attractive and even humorous plates without noticing that the rest of the party had gone downstairs. I felt quite spellbound being able to converse with him about painting, which we both like; and I think that, as we share the same tastes, we would be able to exchange lots of ideas. He chats away most agreeably and is perfectly likeable and nice.

He has to go and see *Iphigénie en Tauride* with M. Degas on Friday. We have already asked Drogue to get seats for us at one of the performances but I fear it won't be the same one as M. Degas and Ernest—it would have been so nice to meet him there.

I went home completely under Ernest's spell, happy to have seen him, and only wishing I had invited him to come and see the paintings at home.

Wednesday 13th December

Drogue has written to say he's taken a box for *Iphigénie* for Friday! I am enchanted. . .

Envoi

Julie interrupted her diary at the end of 1899, probably because she had become engaged and was too busy preparing for her forthcoming marriage to Ernest. The double wedding—Julie and Ernest Rouart, Jeannie Gobillard and Paul Valéry—was, from family accounts, a very jolly affair and had its humorous moments. The elderly gardeners and servants from Le Mesnil had been especially invited to come up to Paris for the occasion but, having no idea of the accustomed etiquette and seeing the wedding breakfast invitingly laid out, promptly sat down and were about to devour the feast before the ceremony; also some confusion reigned in the church with regard to the seating plans and the Mesnil contingent were found sitting in the seats reserved for the bridal couples at the altar. Afterwards Julie and Ernest made their way to Saint-Valéry-en-Caux in Normandy, a small fishing port and popular resort between Fécamp and Dieppe, often painted by Jongkind and Isabey. Berthe Morisot had painted a portrait of her sister Edma in 1873 on the cliffs of the Petites Dalles near by. '*Un endroit absolument sinistre*' was Julie's verdict on this coastal village (recommended by Degas who was not a great traveller himself and, what is more, hated the countryside and the sea). The Valérys were meanwhile honeymooning in Brussels and Amsterdam and the attraction of a cultural stay there soon made Julie and Ernest waste no more time in joining them in Brussels in a quickly improvised *honeymoon-à-quatre*. But very soon they all suffered remorse at having left Paule on her own in Paris and wrote to ask her to join them. Apparently this *honeymoon-à-cinq* was a great success and they returned refreshed and happy to pursue their artistic careers. Julie and Ernest moved in to the fourth-floor apartment at the Rue de Villejust, while Paule, Jeannie and her husband remained on the third floor.

Eventually the Rouarts undertook the restoration and redecoration of the Château du Mesnil, where Julie and Ernest both painted murals in the ground-floor salons. Julie was to bring up her three sons—Julien, Clément and Denis—there, sharing her time between the château and the Rue de Villejust for the remainder of her life, entertaining lifelong friends like Jeanne Baudot and making many new friends among the young artists and poets of the period. Ernest was called up during World War I and served in the army, but, after being gassed on the front in 1917, his health was seriously affected and he became a semi-invalid for the rest of his life.

Ernest and Julie helped organize many important exhibitions including the centenary exhibition for Manet at the Tuileries in 1932, the Degas exhibition in 1937, and the important Berthe Morisot show of 1941. They both painted continuously and lived for art and pictures. Julie tried new techniques; the most successful of these were perhaps the series of plates she decorated with insects and butterflies towards the end of her life. Her god-daughter Agathe Valéry-Rouart remembers her as a calm, serious woman who spoke very slowly and very

*Julie Manet's wedding photograph. On the left, Ernest and Julie; on the right, Paul Valéry and
Jeannie Gobillard. Taken in May 1900 at the Rue de Villejust*

deliberately about art and literature. Her husband on the other hand was of a nervous and quick-tempered disposition—a true Rouart. After his death in 1942 Julie continued to live as before, surrounded by her children and grandchildren until she herself died peacefully in 1966. She had taken up her diary again soon after her marriage but it was no longer the day-to-day journal of a young Parisian girl in the 1890s; it was more introspective as she became an increasingly devout and fervent Catholic.

Madame Ernest Rouart, née Julie Manet, and her firstborn son Julien

*Ernest Rouart and his three
sons, c. 1916*

*The Rouart and Valéry
families, with Paule Gobillard
in the foreground, at Le Mesnil
in 1916. Ernest Rouart is in
uniform*

Julie lived a very pleasant life and she was ever thankful for her blessings. It is this optimistic and heart-warming attitude to life that makes her diary a valuable and extraordinary document, permitting the reader to have a highly personal insight into the lives of the many famous people who made up the artistic and literary Paris of *La Belle Epoque*. It is thanks to Julie's three children, two of whom are still living, that this document has been preserved, and that we are now able to enjoy a measure of Julie Manet's *Journal* in the extracts given here.

Julie Manet, towards the end of her life, in her appartment in the Rue de Villejust

Abridged genealogy of the Morisot and Manet families

Edme-Tiburce Morisot = Marie-Cornélie Thomas
1806–74   1819–76

Yves Morisot
1838–93
married
Théodore Gobillard
b. 1833

Edma Morisot
1840–1921
married
Adolphe Pontillon
d. 1894

Berthe Morisot
1841–95
married
Eugène Manet
1834–92

Tiburce Morisot
b. 1848

Jeanne Pontillon
d. 1921

Blanche
1871–1941
married
Pierre Forget

Edme
b. 1878

Julie Manet
1878–1966
married
Ernest Rouart
1874–1942

Paule Gobillard
1867–1946

Marcel
d. 1921/2

Jeannie
1877–1970
married
Paul Valéry
1871–1945

Julien Rouart
b. 1901

Clément
b. 1906
married
Victoria Rapin

Denis
1908–84
married
Annie Conan

Claude Valéry
b. 1903

Agathe
b. 1906
married
Paul Rouart
1906–72

François
b. 1916

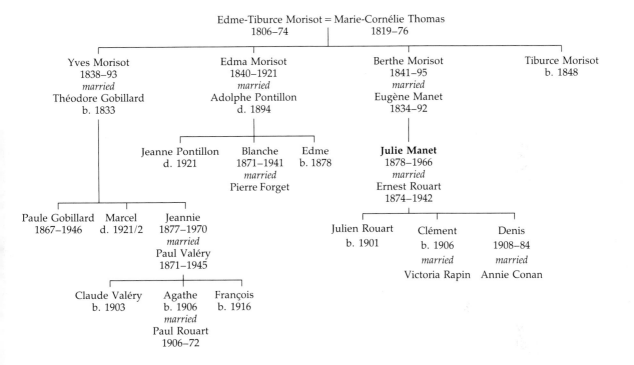

Clément Manet
1764–1814

Auguste Manet = Eugénie Fournier
1796–1862

Edouard Manet
1832–83
married
Suzanne Leenhoff
1830–1906

Eugène = Berthe Morisot
1834–92   1841–95

Julie Manet

Gustave
1835–84

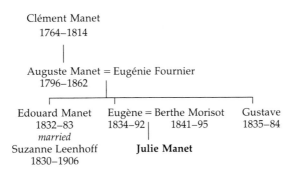

List of names, places and events

Tsar Alexander II (1818–81), responsible for the abolition of slavery in 1861 and the reform of archaic laws in Russia. Assassinated by Nihilists.

Tsar Alexander III (1845–94), son of Alexander II, he was responsible for the Franco-Russian military agreement of 1892. The French named one of their grandest Parisian bridges after him.

Arsène Alexandre, art critic and defender of Toulouse-Lautrec.

The Angoulvent family were friends of the Morisot-Manet households. Monique Angoulvent wrote the first serious biography of Berthe Morisot in 1933, for which Julie Manet provided most of the information.

Louis Anquetin (1861–1932), painter.

Zacharie Astruc (1833–1907), poet, painter, sculptor, critic, and one of the earliest collectors of Japanese art in Paris.

Paul-Albert Bartholomé (1848–1928), painter turned sculptor and one of Degas' best friends.

Marie Bashkirtseff (1860–84), young Russian painter and writer who exhibited at the Salon and worked in a realist style close to that of Jules Bastien-Lepage (with whom she was romantically linked). Her outspoken *Journal*, which was published in 1887 after her death from consumption, was widely read and discussed by artists.

Jeanne Baudot (1877–1957), a doctor's daughter who became an accomplished painter under the guidance of Renoir. She settled in Louveciennes when still in her twenties and was a close friend of Julie Manet, often visiting her at the Château du Mesnil.

Bellevue (Seine-et-Oise, in the Versailles district): in 1748 Jean Cailleteau (Mme de Pompadour's architect) constructed a château at Bellevue, which was decorated by Van Loo, Boucher, and Coustou. During the Revolution it was pillaged and later largely destroyed under the Restoration of 1823. The residential quarter was built over what used to be the park of the château.

Jacques-Emile Blanche (1861–1941), painter, critic, and author who was much influenced by Manet. He painted mainly portraits of society women and literary figures.

Pierre Bonnard (1867–1947), a painter of Intimist compositions (of nudes and interiors especially) with bold use of colour and, with Vuillard, a leading member of the Nabis group.

Doctor Bonniot a member of the Bonniot family from Nantes, who married Geneviève Mallarmé, the poet's daughter.

Jean-Stanislas Jules Boissière (1863–97), French diplomat in Tonkin and Annam, Boissière was one of the first French writers to make a study of the effects of opium in the colonial world. His *Fumeurs d'Opium* was published by Flammarion in 1896.

Mary Cassatt (1844–1926), Impressionist painter, ex-patriate American and friend of Degas.

Paul Cézanne (1839–1906), exhibited with the Impressionists but remained apart from them in artistic terms; his preoccupation with form, modelling, and perspective led his art to the brink of abstraction. Rejected time after time by the Salon juries, Cézanne's deep commitment to his work coupled with his serious nature and difficult temperament caused him to live and work in isolation at Aix for much of his career, though he received visits there from Renoir, Berthe Morisot, and other painters. Cézanne began to achieve great success in the final years of his life and his art has had a far-reaching and profound effect.

Alexis Emmanuel Chabrier (1841–94), composer, befriended by Manet, Berthe Morisot, Verlaine, and Fauré.

Victor Choquet, a customs official and early collector of paintings by Renoir and Cézanne.

Georges Clemenceau (1841–1929), important statesman and friend of the Impressionists who was painted by Manet. He was an opponent of MacMahon and then an ardent Dreyfusard.

Zoë Closier, Degas' last housekeeper, was renowned for her terrible cooking and complained that M. Degas preferred to spend money on an Ingres drawing rather than give her a proper housekeeping allowance. She was invaluable to him in many ways—reading to him, running errands, and deterring unwanted visitors.

The Commune: the revolutionary 'people's power' which took control of Paris in March 1871 after the withdrawal of triumphant Prussian troops. In protest against the acceptance of the harsh terms imposed on France, it was founded by left-wing National guardsmen and Republican citizens to resist the weak government of Thiers. Civil war raged for several weeks in siege conditions, with many public buildings (seen as symbols of right-wing authority) being destroyed and over 20,000 Parisians being killed. Eventually, in May, government forces under MacMahon supressed the uprising.

Concerts Colonne: music association founded by Edouard Colonne (1838–1910), a distinguished violinist and conductor who was a passionate enthusiast of French composers such as Berlioz, Bizet, Gounod and, later, Ravel and Debussy.

Concerts Lamoureux: founded by Charles Lamoureux (1834–99), who was a Wagner enthusiast and who was the first musician to conduct the Ring Cycle in France.

Jean-Baptiste Corot (1796–1875), major French landscape artist of the first half of the nineteenth century, said to be the first to work *en plein air* though he studied with the neo-classical Michallon and Bertin. He advised and helped many young artists, among them Berthe Morisot.

Claude Debussy (1862–1918), composer who collaborated with many of the poets of the period, including Baudelaire, Mallarmé, and Maeterlinck.

Hilaire-Germain Edgar (de Gas) Degas (1834–1917), French painter who came from a wealthy and highly cultivated background. However, unlike most of his fellow Impressionists, he was not a painter of nature, taking his inspiration instead from the theatre (ballet in particular), horse racing, and portraiture. He was fascinated by the new art of photography and used the camera as a means of recording subjects for later inclusion in his compositions. Degas' œuvre came very close to the Naturalism espoused by Zola. Whilst undoubtedly a very great painter in his own right, Degas had very little influence on other artists in his lifetime or since, and he was largely unaffected by the tremendous changes taking place in art in the late nineteenth century.

Eugène Delacroix (1799–1863), leading painter of the Romantic school who influenced the Impressionists by his free use of colour and impasto, his exotic subjects, and his passion for light and movement in painting. His diary is still read by the serious artist and art historian.

Jules-Elie Delaunay (1828–91), painter and teacher at the Ecole des Beaux-Arts known for his frescoes for the Opéra.

Maurice Denis (1870–1943), important Symbolist and religious artist, friend of Gauguin and Sérusier, and founder member of the Nabis group.

Marceline Desbordes-Valmore (1785–1859), writer, particularly known for her inspirational elegiac poetry.

The Dreyfus Affair: Capitaine Alfred Dreyfus (1859–1935), a French army officer and a Jew, was condemned by military secret tribunal in 1894 (on a false charge of divulging secrets to the German government) to life imprisonment on Devil's Island, French Guiana. A sensational new trial in 1899 again found him guilty but the sentence was reduced to ten years. Later in that same year Dreyfus accepted a clemency offer by President Emile Loubet. But it was not until 1906, when anti-Semitism had died down somewhat, that the verdict was reversed and Dreyfus was entirely exonerated and reinstated in the army.

Jacques Drogue appears many times in the diary but very little is known about him other than the fact that he seems to have been an entertaining and amusing friend.

Carolus Duran (Charles Durand) (1837–1917), a painter, influenced by Spanish art and Velasquez in particular, who admired Courbet also. He was an important Academic and fashionable portraitist.

Durand-Ruel Gallery: the Durand-Ruel family had developed their modest stationery business on the Left Bank to become fashionable art dealers on the Rue de la Paix, exhibiting Delacroix, Corot, Daumier, and the Barbizon painters. Paul Durand-Ruel, son of the founder, took over the business in 1865 and expanded to even larger premises in the Rue Laffitte and the Rue Le Peletier (near Garnier's new Opera House). In 1870, because of the Franco-Prussian war, Durand-Ruel moved his stock to London (168 New Bond Street), where he exhibited not only Manet and Degas but also Monet and Pissarro, both in exile there at that time. By the 1890s Durand-Ruel had shown most of the major Impressionists and was therefore a natural choice for the Berthe Morisot retrospective in 1896.

Théodore Duret, wealthy cognac dealer, Republican journalist, and art critic, who became an apologist for the Avant-garde when he published his pamphlet on the Impressionist painters. His collection of works by all the major artists of his time was dispersed in 1894.

Georges d'Espagnat (1870–1950), painter.

Jules Abel Faivre (1867–1945), painter turned caricaturist who worked for a time with Renoir but attained fame by illustrating such periodicals as *L'Assiette au Beurre* and *Le Rire*.

Henri Fantin-Latour (1836–1904), *intimiste* painter, friend and defender of Manet; best known as a flower painter and interpreter of musical themes.

Léon-Paul Fargue (1876–1947), Mallarmé's most ardent disciple; friend of André Gide and Paul Valéry.

The Fashoda Incident: this 'exploded' in 1898 and left a feeling of hostility in France towards England and the English. Fashoda, a village on the Nile, was in territory claimed by both France and the British on behalf of Egypt and was occupied by Général Marchand leading a French expedition from the Congo. Kitchener, victor of Omdurman, invited Marchand to retire, but he refused to do so without orders from the French government. Much excitement was aroused, rumours of war between the two countries being frequent. Eventually the French government, facing an already difficult split in their country over the Dreyfus Affair, ordered Marchand to withdraw. In 1899 the British granted the French certain desert areas in the Sahara in lieu of Fashoda but anti-British feeling remained strong for some time. Fashoda was renamed Kodok in 1904.

Félix Faure (1841–99), wealthy leather merchant from Le Havre who was elected president of the Third Republic by the moderate coalition in January 1895. He was in office during the period of most of Julie's diary.

Jean-Louis Forain (1852–1931), painter of contemporary life and newspaper illustrator, who studied with Gérôme but whose main influences were Degas, Daumier, Manet, and Toulouse-Lautrec.

Forest of Fontainebleau and Barbizon: it was in this area that Corot and his pupils came to paint in the open air in the 1850s and '60s. The picturesque village of Barbizon gave its name to the school of landscapists, which included Théodore Rousseau, François Daubigny, and Diaz de la Peña. These artists were to have a direct influence on the Impressionists.

The Français (the Théâtre-Français or the Comédie-Française): founded in 1680 by order of Louis XIV. Dissolved in 1792 because of the French Revolution, it was recreated in 1804 and has been the centre of French theatrical tradition ever since.

Loïe Fuller (1862–1928), American dancer at the Folies Bergère who was painted by Toulouse Lautrec and Jean-Louis Forain.

Paul Gallimard was a Paris impresario with a large Renoir collection who once owned the Théâtre des Variétés.

Léon Gambetta (1838–82), distinguished left-wing statesman who was MacMahon's main opponent. His career spanned the Franco-Prussian war, the Commune, and the creation of his own party (L'Union Républicaine).

Paul Gauguin (1848–1903), after a childhood spent partly in Peru and an early life as a sailor, then a career in finance, became a full-time painter in 1883. He left his wife and children to travel, firstly to Pont-Aven in Brittany, then farther afield to Martinique, Tahiti, and finally to the Marquesas Islands where he died.

Gustave Geffroy (1855–1926), novelist and art critic.

Giverny: Monet's country property at Giverny near the Seine which he acquired in 1890 and where he lived for the last years of his life. It is notable especially for the water garden which inspired Monet's *Nymphéas* pictures.

Joseph-Albert Glatigny (1839–73), comedian, actor, journalist, and dramatist as well as poet, whose amusing though facile poetic juggling suffused satire with spontaneous inspiration.

Eva Gonzalès (1849–83), painter, who studied with Manet and exhibited at the Salon from 1870–83. She married the etcher Henri Guérard in 1879 but died in childbirth at the age of 33.

Adolphe Goupil, Parisian art collector and dealer whose firm dated back to 1827. He had three important galleries in the centre of Paris and branches in New York, London, Berlin, Brussels, Vienna, and The Hague. Goupil was for some time the employer of Vincent van Gogh, whose brother Theo became a director from 1878. In 1885 the firm was renamed by Boussod and Valadon. Maurice Joyant took over its management after Theo van Gogh's death in 1891.

Charles Haviland, porcelain manufacturer at Limoges and Auteuil. He was a great friend of Renoir, who painted his son Paul in 1884. After World War I he supplied Julie Manet with the porcelain which she used to decorate.

Paul-César Helleu (1859–1927), painter and sculptor, pupil of Gérôme, who specialized in portraits of the elegant women of the *Belle Epoque*.

José-Maria de Heredia (1842–1905), Cuban by birth but essentially a French poet; disciple of Leconte de Lisle and friend of Catulle Mendès.

La Libre Esthétique: Avant-garde art gallery in Brussels.

La Libre Parole: anti-Semitic newspaper.

Charles Leconte de Lisle (1818–94), French poet born on the island of La Réunion and founder member of the Parnassian school of poetry.

Henri Lerolle (1848–1921), painter who formed a bridge between the traditionalists and the Indépendants, with friends among both groups. He is known for his murals in the Sorbonne and in the church of St-Martin-des-Champs, Paris. His daughter Yvonne was a close friend of Julie Manet and her cousins.

Pierre Louÿs (1870–1925), French man of letters and poet, married to José-Maria de Heredia's daughter, and friend of Paul Valéry, Debussy, and Honneger.

Comte Marie Edme MacMahon (1808–193), Grand Marshal of France and distinguished statesman. After an exemplary military career, in 1873 he was elected second president of the Third Republic by the Monarchist coalition, an office he held until a Republican majority forced his resignation.

Comte Maurice Maeterlinck (1862–1949), Belgian naturalist, poet, and dramatist, who won the Nobel Prize for Literature in 1911.

Stéphane Mallarmé (1842–98), poet who launched the Symbolist movement. He met Berthe Morisot through his friend Manet, who had painted his portrait in 1876. Mallarmé and Berthe Morisot became great friends and when she died in 1895 he became Julie's guardian.

Edouard Manet (1832–83), Julie's uncle, more than any other artist of his generation, was the major driving force behind a new way of thinking about art which began in the 1860s. He was the pivot around which modern art was born; and, while he attracted the hostility and scorn of public and critics alike, he was championed by his mainly younger contemporaries including Monet, Renoir, Cézanne and Pissarro, who considered him their leader. His work created public scandals, beginning with the Salon entry (rejected by the jury), DÉJEUNER SUR L'HERBE, of 1863, which was subsequently hung in the Salon des Refusés and created a furore among visitors to the exhibition. Manet, a wit, dandy and *flaneur des boulevards* from a wealthy bourgeois family, nonetheless sought official recognition and acceptance, which he was denied until late in his career. He was steadfast in his refusal to exhibit with the Impressionists, though he worked alongside them in the early 1870s, and he had a close and lasting relationship with Berthe Morisot (who became his sister-in-law in 1874). Manet died at the age of 51, prematurely, like his two brothers.

Camille Mauclair (1872–1945), poet, author, and critic. He succeeded Albert Aurier as art critic of *Mercure de France* in 1893.

Catulle Mendès (1841–1909), disciple of Théophile Gautier and Villiers de l'Isle-Adam, he was a Germanophile and ardent admirer of Wagner. A founder member of the Parnassian school of poetry, he wrote many lyrics for operas and operetta, especially for Chabrier.

Octave Mirbeau (1850–1917), controversial novelist, dramatist, and journalist who developed from being ultra Royalist and Catholic into a passionate anarchist and anti-Semitist.

Frédéric Mistral (1830–1914), the great Provençal poet who was responsible for the establishment of the Provençal language (*la lange d'Oc*) as a literary medium. He was a friend of many of the Impressionists and was also an ardent anti-Dreyfusard. Joint winner of the Nobel prize for literature in 1904.

Claude Monet (1840–1926), founder member and recognized as one of the greatest of the Impressionist group. He spent his childhood in Le Havre, went to Paris in 1859, and met Camille Pissarro at the Atelier Suisse. He knew Manet by 1866 but it is not certain when he met Berthe Morisot. By the time Julie began her diary he was already an established figure. His second wife, Alice Hoschedé-Monet, was first married to Ernest Hoschedé. In 1878 she and her six children came to live with the Monets at Vétheuil, after the bankruptcy of her husband, and she continued to live with Monet after the death of his wife Camille, marrying him in 1892.

Gustave Moreau (1826–98), Symbolist painter and teacher at the Ecole des Beaux-Arts where his most noted students were Marquet, Matisse, and Roualt. Degas disliked his paintings, and compared them to masses of watch-chains (*chaines de montres*).

Edma Morisot (1840–94), sister of Berthe, married Adolphe Pontillon, a naval officer, and gave up painting. Her two daughters were Jeanne and Blanche; her son, Edme.

Yves Morisot (1838–93), sister of Berthe, married Paul Théodore Gobillard, a tax official, and had three children—Paule, Marcel, and Jeannie.

Thadée Natanson, publisher and editor of *La Revue Blanche*; he and his wife Misia were influential members of Parisian society.

Tsar Nicholas II (1868–1918), son of Alexander III and last tsar of Russia, came to the throne in 1894. He supported the Franco-Russian Alliance by making a ceremonial visit to France in 1896, receiving President Félix Faure in return in Russia the following year. Executed by the Bolsheviks.

Georges Petit, important Parisian art dealer who took over the long-established family firm in 1878 and exhibited the Impressionists. In 1882 he opened a large gallery near the Madeleine in competition with Durand-Ruel.

Camille Pissarro (1830–1903), landscapist, of Portuguese-Jewish-Creole descent. He studied under Corot and was fellow Impressionist and friend of Monet and Renoir. His eldest son Lucien was also a painter.

Raymond Poincaré (1860–1934), president of France from 1913–20 and several times prime minister. He refused to take sides in the Dreyfus Affair.

Pont-Aven: a picturesque village in Finistère, Brittany, where Gauguin, Denis, Emile Bernard, and Paul Sérusier painted in the late 1880s and which gave its name to their group.

Pierre Puvis de Chavannes (1824–98), a leading Symbolist muralist and painter in the classical tradition, friend of Degas and the Impressionists, who frequently visited Berthe Morisot and attended her soirées.

Odilon Redon (1840–1916), Symbolist painter of semi-Impressionist style, often of vases of flowers and also fantastic subjects.

Henri de Régnier (1864–1936), Symbolist poet and member of the Parnassians.

Pierre Auguste Renoir (1841–1919), a leading member of the Impressionist group. He was a pupil of Gleyre and a friend of Monet, Bazille, and Sisley. It is difficult to determine when he first met Berthe Morisot—their close friendship dated from the 1880s. His wife was the former Aline Charigot (1868–1915).

Léon Riesener (1808–78), painter, and pupil of Delacroix. His daughter Rosalie was a friend and model of Berthe Morisot.

Stanislas Henri Rouart (1833–1912), schoolfriend of Degas and amateur painter who studied with Millet and Corot and exhibited at the Salon. He was head of a successful metallurgical enterprise and a notable art collector. Ernest Rouart, his artist son, was a pupil of Degas and future husband of Julie Manet.

Russians: in October 1893 there was an official visit of Russian warships to France. They arrived at Toulon on 13th October and the officers were officially welcomed to Paris on 17th October with a dinner and ball at the Elysée Palace. Over the next few days they attended a torchlight procession through the streets of Paris, a banquet on the Champ-de-Mars, river fêtes, a fireworks display and many other engagements before leaving on 24th. It was during this visit that the funeral of MacMahon took place (on the 22nd).

Salon: name given to the exhibitions of the French Royal Academy of Painting and Sculpture (founded in the seventeenth century) held in the Salon d'Apollon in the Louvre. Known as the 'Salon Officiel' after the Revolution. When the annual exhibitions outgrew the Louvre they were moved to the Palais de l'Industrie, built in 1854 in the Champs-Elysées. After the Palais de l'Industrie was torn down in 1900 the Salon moved across the river and the Grand and Petit Palais were built on its site.

Salon became a general word to describe a group exhibition in Paris and, apart from the official Salon, reorganized in 1881 as the Société des Artistes Français, there were several others of importance:

The Salon des Refusés where over two thousand artists rejected by the official Salon jury in 1863 exhibited works at the Palais des Champs-Elysées. This 'counter salon' became a fashionable and slightly *risqué* place to be seen and opened two weeks after the official one but public opposition was so great that it was not repeated as such.

The Salon des Indépendants created in 1884 by another large group of rejected artists such as Seurat.

The more esoteric Salon de la Nationale, sometimes called the Salon du Champ-de-Mars, founded in the 1890s by the painter Puvis de Chavannes which concentrated on Symbolist works.

Alfred Sisley (1839–99), French Impressionist of English origin who was a friend of Monet and Renoir. He worked particularly along the banks of the Seine at Louveciennes and Bougival and at Moret-sur-Loing.

Alfred Stevens (1828–1906), Belgian portrait and genre painter, and member of the Morisot-Manet circle. In 1886 Stevens published his successful *Impressions sur la Peinture*. Sarah Bernhardt was one of the many women who studied at his atelier.

Gabriel Thomas (1854–1932), a businessman and cousin of Berthe Morisot who was especially interested in the arts. He was made deputy administrator of the Musée Grevin in 1883 and was responsible for its historical reconstruction. As president of the Société de la Tour Eiffel, he was associated in the invention of a moving stairway at the 1900 Exposition Universelle. He directed the building of the Théâtre des Champs-Elysées, and in 1924 conceived the idea of having illuminated advertising on the Eiffel Tower. He also patented a type of theatre lighting. A bibliophile and art collector, he was involved in fine art publishing with Maurice Denis.

Valadon—see Adolphe Goupil.

Paul Valéry (1871–1945), poet and philosopher of French and Italian parentage, protégé of Mallarmé, elected to the Académie Française in 1917. Future husband of Jeannie Gobillard.

Comte Phillipe Auguste Villiers de l'Isle-Adam (1840–89), Symbolist poet and author who died almost unknown and unread, although his work was admired by poets and especially his friends Mallarmé and Baudelaire.

Ambroise Vollard (1868–1939), Creole art dealer born in Saint Denis, Île de la Réunion, who had premises in the Rue Laffitte where he exhibited Avant-garde artists.

Albert Wolff (1835–91), French writer and dramatist of German descent who was sometime theatre critic of *Le Figaro*. A hostile review of his on the 1876 Impressionist Exhibition referred to Berthe Morisot as a lunatic, after which it was reported that Eugène Manet had to be prevented from challenging Wolff to a duel.

Teodore de Wyzewa (1862–1917), art collector, critic, and writer of Polish origin who admired Mallarmé and Berthe Morisot. He was obsessively anti-Dreyfusard.

Federico Zandomeneghi (1841–1917), Italian painter born in Venice into a family of sculptors. Fought under Garibaldi before coming to Paris in 1874. He exhibited with the Impressionists.

Emile Zola (1840–1902), the novelist who was the leading exponent of naturalism in French literature. From early on he was a contributor to various newspapers and journals, and wrote many articles on painting including *Mon Salon* and *Edouard Manet* (Manet was a close friend). Anti-clerical, anti-monarchist and anti-military, he was convinced that Dreyfus had been wrongly accused and succeeded in his attempt to secure a retrial. But on 23rd February 1898 he was sentenced to a year's imprisonment and a fine of 3,000 francs for libelling the court-martial which tried and acquitted Major Esterhazy in the Dreyfus Affair in his *J'Accuse*, published in *L'Aurore*. The sentence was annulled but a retrial returned the same verdict, forcing Zola into temporary exile in England.

Julie aged about 30

Acknowledgements

The authors would like to thank the following for their kind permission to reproduce the works illustrated in this book:

Agence Sygma, Paris pp. 97, 99, 101, 102, 103, 122

Archives Durand-Ruel p. 85

Bibliothèque Nationale, Paris pp. 44, 61, 79, 81, 84, 105

Editions du Seuil, Paris pp. 30, 31, 33, 73, 143

Faber & Faber, R.H. Wilenski, Modern French Painters, London 1957: p. 40

Metropolitan Museum of Art, New York pp. 10, 77 (bequest of Mrs H.C. Havemeyer)

Musée du Louvre, Cabinet des Dessins p. 91

Musée Marmottan, Paris p. 29

Musée d'Orsay, Paris pp. 131, 137

Private collections pp. 2, 4, 7, 8, 13, 14, 15, 16, 17, 18, 19, 20, 21, 23, 26, 33, 35, 39, 41, 43, 45, 47, 48, 51, 53, 55, 56, 59, 60, 66, 69, 70, 71, 78, 80, 87, 96, 106, 109, 111, 115, 125, 131, 135, 141, 144, 149, 150, 155, 156, 163, 164, 166, 168, 169, 170, 177, 179, 181, 183, 184, 187, 188, 190, 192, 193, 194, 195

Rhode Island School of Design, Providence, Rhode Island p. 82

Roger-Viollet, Paris pp. 36, 38, 77, 153

Vendredi 27 Janvier — Séance
Bugno Ysaye consacrée à Bach. La
dernière Sonate qu'ils jouent en la majeur
est un délice. J'aime cette musique
de Bach si précise.
Nous sommes toutes étonnées de trouver
Mr Lerolle qui nous dit que Christine ne
va pas mai.

Samedi 28 Janvier. Chez Mr Degas
pour lui demander de faire un dessin
pour publier avec les poésies de Mr
Mallarmé ; mais naturellement il refuse
puisque c'est publié par des Dreyfusards.
Étant donné ses idées je le comprends un
peu. Il nous montre la nature
morte de Delacroix qu'il vient d'acheter
et le portrait d'Ingres par lui même.
Il nous charge de bien des choses pour